Alfred Fagon Selected Plays

Alfred Fagon Selected Plays

A Day in the Bristol Air Raid Shelter
Adventure Inside Thirteen
Four Hundred Pounds
No Soldiers in St Paul's
Shakespeare Country
Small World
Weekend Lovers

ALFRED FAGON

methuen | drama
LONDON • NEW YORK • OXFORD • NEW DELHI • SYDNEY

METHUEN DRAMA
Bloomsbury Publishing Plc
50 Bedford Square, London, WC1B 3DP, UK
1385 Broadway, New York, NY 10018, USA
29 Earlsfort Terrace, Dublin 2, Ireland

BLOOMSBURY, METHUEN DRAMA and the Methuen Drama logo are trademarks
of Bloomsbury Publishing Plc

First published in Great Britain 2023

A catalogue record for this book is available from the British Library.

A catalog record for this book is available from the Library of Congress.

ISBN: HB: 978-1-3502-7084-8
       PB: 978-1-3502-7083-1
       ePDF: 978-1-3502-7085-5
       eBook: 978-1-3502-7086-2

Typeset RefineCatch Limited, Bungay, Suffolk

To find out more about our authors and books visit www.bloomsbury.com
and sign up for our newsletters.

Contents

Foreword by Dawn Walton OBE vii

A Day in the Bristol Air Raid Shelter 1

Adventure Inside Thirteen 33

Four Hundred Pounds 75

No Soldiers in St Paul's 95

Shakespeare Country 123

Small World 141

Weekend Lovers 195

Reflections by Alfred Fagon Award Winner – Juliet Gilkes Romero 209

Foreword

The first time I heard the name Alfred Fagon was back in 2000 when the winner of the Alfred Fagon Awards was announced. My 'Who is Alfred Fagon?' was met with a detailed description of the tragic circumstances surrounding Alfred's untimely death of a heart attack aged only forty-nine, and the subsequent failure of the police to identify his body leading to an anonymous burial. There were fewer details about his writing or productions.

I attempted to find out more about Alfred Fagon and turned to the internet but Ask Jeeves (yes it was pre-Google) had nothing. Hardly surprising as there is an undocumented history of Black British theatre that is full to the brim with writers, actors, directors and other creatives all long forgotten.

Twenty years later I recalled that conversation when I was contacted by the artistic director of Hampstead Theatre, Roxana Silbert, asking me if I had ever read Fagon's play *The Death of a Black Man*. I had. I read it in his published collection alongside two of his other plays, *11 Josephine House* and *Lonely Cowboy*. Hampstead Theatre was about to celebrate its sixtieth anniversary and had programmed only four plays from its extensive backlist that had received their debut productions at the theatre. I was surprised to learn that Fagon's play *The Death of a Black Man* had its premiere at Hampstead Theatre in a production directed by Roland Rees and starring Mona Hammond, Gregory Munroe and Anton Phillips back in 1975. If I am honest, Hampstead was not a theatre I would have expected to feature in the early history of Black British Theatre. But all credit to the original Foco Novo production for getting a season on in that space. And now I was being asked if I would like to direct its first revival forty-five years later. Personally I had never seen a production of any of Fagon's plays and I felt strongly that theatre needed to honour its pioneers. And I had no doubt that Alfred Fagon was a weighty pioneer whose work should be known widely. So it wasn't hard to say yes. Here are some other reasons.

Up until the early 1970s 'Black theatre' in Britain was examining and chronicling the stories of 'back home' life in Jamaica (Alfred Fagon's home), Trinidad and other Caribbean countries. Then there were the stories of those who had taken up the invitation and made the journey to the UK to help rebuild Britain in the post-war years whilst still yearning for 'home'. Playwrights like Errol John, Barry Reckord, Michael Abbensetts and Mustapha Matura all had plays exploring those themes and settings. Even Fagon takes on the tension between maintaining Caribbean values and the temptations of life in the UK with his first play *11 Josephine House*. Arriving in England from Jamaica at the age of eighteen Fagon would have been all too aware of those tensions.

With *The Death of a Black Man* Fagon created one of the earliest plays to focus on the lives of the *children* of the 'Windrush generation' in Britain. All three of the characters are first-generation British born (or educated) with a Jamaican heritage. But there is no talk of 'back home'. Jamaica is not on their minds. They are already home. They are all aspirational and they are all negotiating their way up the social ladder in England with full knowledge of the position of Black communities at the time.

Fagon sets *The Death of a Black Man* in 1973, so it sits in the middle of a decade which begins with Enoch Powell's anti-immigration 'Rivers of Blood' speech (1968) and the rise of Margaret Thatcher (1979) with her focus on individual social mobility and her denial of 'society'. (I have no doubt that Fagon set out to write a deeply political play.)

1973 is also significant as it was a year that the West Indies cricket team beat England 2-0 in the Test series. The colonised beating the colonisers at their own game. 1973 is also the year the Notting Hill Carnival grew in size and featured its first sound system, after originally starting in 1966 – still one of the biggest celebrations of Blackness/ Caribbean heritage in Europe. These two events indicate a growing sense of Black confidence and Fagon uses this metaphor to start the play

The entire play is set in a swanky flat in Chelsea which the stage directions tell us is 'furnished in Habitat style'.

There are three characters and the story plays out over four acts.

In the opening prologue we find the owner of the flat – eighteen-year-old Shakie – is London-born with a working-class background. He is dressed in army uniform and holding a cricket bat. He delivers a direct address that celebrates the West Indian cricket team, especially Garfield Sobers, and the Notting Hill Carnival in unabashed Black boy joy. Even today in theatre this is a rare and a provocative scene. It completely confounds the stereotype of a young Black man.

Furthermore Shakie is a superb businessman selling African arts and crafts (imported from Yorkshire) to the American 'beatniks' on the King's Road and is making enough money for the flat, tailored suits and a fridge that is always full of champagne. He is fully assimilated in his Chelsea home and his goal is to get rich as fast as possible. He will use any attribute to get it.

Jackie is aged thirty; she is Shakie's ex-girlfriend and mother of Shakie's child. She is Jamaican-born but educated in an English private boarding school, suggesting that she has come from a rich family, but there is no evidence that Jackie has any means of her own. In the UK her social mobility comes from her education. Although there are plenty of clues there is a lot more mystery around this character and it could be said that Fagon was less successful with this characterisation.

Stumpie is aged nineteen and best friend to Shakie. The two young men grew up together in the same streets/estate in London but there is a hint that Stumpie may have arrived in the UK as a small child. He has been away travelling around Europe and Africa and has returned with the politics of Pan-Africanism and Black power that had started to influence Black communities in the 1960s. He wants his friend to fund his dream business of bringing African musicians to the UK.

I cannot imagine what it must have been like on opening night in that theatre. These characters completely confounded the popular stereotypes of young Black British people in the mid-1970s. Not having the living playwright or most of his contemporaries to refer to and finding little or no documentation, I leaned into Fagon's text for clues to help with this new production.

Mustapha Matura was a friend and colleague of Fagon's. There is a story that working actor Alfred Fagon was auditioning for a part in one of Matura's plays and was amazed that the characters were written as they really spoke, including their authentic patois. It is said that he started writing plays after he discovered that this wasn't forbidden on stage.

He found it easy to write. Like the very best playwrights Fagon had an ear for dialogue and was perfectly placed to put challenging Black voices onstage. *The Death of a Black Man* has the messiness of real speech, full of repetition and circular arguments. This is exaggerated at points when alcohol or weed is involved. I spent a lot of time alone in a room reading *The Death of a Black Man* out loud so I could hear it. It was written to be spoken as all great plays are. I started to notice that characters had changes in their rhythm. This would even happen mid-sentence.

During the prologue we hear Shakie the Londoner with some patois thrown in. He is interrupted by Jackie walking into his flat and his language and rhythm instantly changes:

Jackie   Not even glad to see me?

Shakie   I am flabbergasted.

Jackie   Don't worry, I'm on holiday. Only passing through. Two years ago was the last time I saw you.

Shakie   It was the same time I last saw you too.

Shakie *matches* **Jackie**'s *more clipped middle-class delivery and reveals himself to be an expert in 'code switching'.* **Shakie**'s *language and rhythm shifts again when* **Stumpie** *arrives this time shifting from London to Jamaican patois.*

Stumpie   Hippies!

Shakie   No. Rass clath beatniks!

It makes total sense that aspirational super-salesman Shakie would have code switching in his toolbox. He needs to move across race, class and age in order to do business successfully.

Stumpie uses his code switch to emphasise his politics and to alienate Jackie. Jackie doesn't need a code switch.

The dynamics between the three characters – two men and one woman – has led many to suggest that Alfred Fagon was influenced by Harold Pinter. Indeed Pinter's *The Dumb Waiter* was also programmed in the Hampstead Theatre anniversary season. I tried to find evidence of this by talking to those in theatre who knew him but no one could confirm that he had even seen a Pinter production. But Fagon's four-act structure was remarkable in that each act had a marked shift in temperature.

Working with a longtime collaborator – the designer Simon Kenny – we spent a lot of time talking about this and reached for a theatrical shorthand. Act One plays like a Noël Coward two-hander. Act Two, with the introduction of Stumpie who is negative to Jackie, has the Pinter influence I have referenced. After the titular event happens offstage between Acts Two and Three there is another shift and Act Three turns into a dream play full of smoke and big ideas. The scale of Act Four suggests Fagon has moved into full operatic proportions. Even though we never leave the single location Kenny reflected this brilliantly in the design by progressively stripping away the walls until the characters are marooned on a menacing island.

With *The Death of a Black Man* Fagon was not afraid to take on big themes: cultural appropriation, race, class, colonialism, religion, capitalism. While Fagon's gender politics is difficult and really challenging for a twenty-first-century sensibility there is no denying the contemporary resonance of his work. And the play is very funny – until it's not appropriate to be.

My revival was originally scheduled before the Covid pandemic but instead we all landed in lockdown. During the 'great isolation' the whole world witnessed the murder of George Floyd at the hands of a police officer. In the second half of *The Death of a Black Man*, when news of the death reaches Shakie's Chelsea flat, the hard politics of the piece comes to the fore. The characters talk about the oppression and murder of Black people in Angola, Mozambique and South Africa, the actions of the male protagonists get more desperate and Jackie becomes more isolated.

Alfred Fagon, soldier, boxing champion, welder, father, actor, poet, playwright, chronicler and soothsayer. Wonderful to see his legacy shared this way.

Thanks to all who have kept his name and his work alive.

I wish I had met him.

Dawn Walton OBE
Director, *The Death of a Black Man* (Hampstead Theatre, 2021)

A Day in the Bristol Air Raid Shelter

Characters

Man
Woman

Man So how long have you been coming to this amazing hole inside another hole?

Woman Longer than I care to remember. I'm a sculptor.

Man So you are an artist since the day you were born?

Woman Yes always. Well, I used to play marbles then I took to chopping down trees. Why did you follow me this morning?

Man I couldn't help myself. I been trying to talk to you for a long time.

Woman Okay so now's your chance.

Man It's not easy is it?

Woman What?

Man Talking to you I mean.

Woman Oh I see. Well, that's your problem.

Man My problem is your problem.

Woman Since when?

Man Since we start talking.

Woman You move quickly.

Man Life is quick.

Woman Yes it is funny the way things happened, sometimes life is full of surprises.

Man You telling me.

Woman So how long have you been watching me?

Man Years and years.

Woman Was it frustrating?

Man I enjoyed it.

Woman Good for you.

Man I don't know about that.

Woman Well, you should since you claim you've been watching me for years.

Man What you think is going to happen in the year two thousand?

Woman It's only 1976.

Man Some people take the year two thousand very, may I tell you very serious indeed.

Woman Well, I don't and you shouldn't worry about other people. The year two thousand's all in the future.

Man Yes you look hard enough not to worry about the year two thousand. I can't make up my mind about the year two thousand, maybe nothing is going to happen in the year two thousand than what is happening in 1976 except doctors might find it easy to say to the enormously insane population two thousand guineas please fuck the please two thousand guineas are you is as good as dead and we will tie your two big toes together with a title on the label deceased gone underground burn the bastard, why are you so serious?

Woman   Looks can be deceiving.

Man   Who do you think you look like to me?

Woman   Are you serious?

Man   No.

Woman   I was up and about early hours this morning in the morning mist gathering energy for the rest of the day.

Man   Me too, my tank is full of mystery energy.

Woman   It's telepathy.

Man   Could be a day to remember.

Woman   I hope so.

Man   What the hell is going on in Bristol?

Woman   You asking me?

Man   I don't know what I want to say to you really.

Woman   Well, you don't have to say if you don't want to.

Man   It's hard to keep your mouth shut isn't it?

Woman   That shouldn't be too hard, just shut it.

Man   True, true.

Woman   But it's not as easy as that is it?

Man   Tell me about your underground work down here.

Woman   There's nothing to tell, just look at them for pleasure.

Man   Why do you walk so fast?

Woman   I wasn't aware that I did.

Man   Oh yes you do, you were even running the other morning.

Woman   Only because it was raining.

Man   I like the rain, do you?

Woman   Yes I do.

Man   You going to give us a cup of tea then?

Woman   I haven't got any tea.

Man   Surprise, surprise.

Woman   You see that piece over there.

Man   Yeah.

Woman   Four years went into that – hard labour.

Man   That's a long prison sentence.

Woman   Yes I know, I like it though there's a lot of me in that.

Man   You make me feel guilty.

Woman   Oh is that so, why?

Man   I don't know. So here we are then.

Woman   Yes, we are here.

Man   I have never done this before.

Woman   Well, do you like my studio?

Man   Yes but everything look like hard work to me.

Woman   Everything is hard work. This is the pieces I am working on at the moment.

Man   They all look the same to me.

Woman   Well, they are not all the same.

Man   How comes?

Woman   How comes what?

Man   You look funny when you are in your studio.

Woman   Well, for your information I don't feel funny.

Man   Can't say I agree with you, there's a lot more light in your face since you came into your studio.

Woman   You don't have to patronise me, I don't particularly like that type of attitude.

Man   Why is artist so frustrated?

Woman   Right, how to do this morning, I can't think straight with you around.

Man   Chop up more wood I suppose.

Woman   Right, stand over there.

Man   What's that, stand where?

Woman   Are you any good at pulling funny faces?

Man   Maybe.

Woman   Well, get some practice in, I'm gonna take some photos.

Man   That's interesting.

Woman   Yes it is.

Man   What are you gonna do with the photos?

Woman   Look at them, what else.

Man   I know that.

Woman   So why did you ask?

Man   Sorry I'm a little bit shaken with your sudden burst of athletic energy.

Woman   Never apologise to anyone, child. Let's get started, first your face.

Man   Sure why not if my face interest you.

Woman   Okay. I don't particularly like the jacket, I don't think it would go well with this shot, take it off.

Man   What else don't you like about my garments?

Woman   I will let you know that in a minute.

Man   I can't wait, I wonder if you would marry me?

Woman   You are wondering about it are you?

Man   Yes.

Woman   Okay, mister, back up against the wall.

Man   If this is a stick-up, I haven't got any money.

Woman   Spread your arms as if you was Jesus on the cross.

Man   Jesus Christ. It's not Good Friday is it, or is it gonna be another lynching?

Woman   You're not that unlucky. Okay, kid, drop your left arm.

Man   Now I know what my right arm's for.

Woman   Stretch your arms in front of you.

Man   What am I now, Moses crossing the Red Sea?

Woman   That's a good one. Right, right, take off your shirt.

Man   Sure thing, what about my trousers?

Woman   You can keep them on for the time being.

Man   Thank you. It's a pleasure to work for you.

Woman   Right, get hold of this with both hands.

Man   Mighty Jehovah Witness, have you any feathers or paint?

Woman   No, you look better without make-up.

Man   I didn't know you were gonna shoot a movie.

Woman   Right, right now I want some good shots, steady with the eyeballs. Where did you say you come from?

Man   I will tell you for the last time.

Woman   No don't. Jamaica, okay, okay. You look like an African to me.

Man   What type, Black or white?

Woman   Oh definitely Black. Good, just imagine you're in the jungle, somewhere in Jamaica or Africa, it doesn't matter which jungle. Good, good. I've always wanted to do this. You must act funny, okay, okay, kid?

Man   Are you enjoying yourself, madam?

Woman   Oh immensely, marvellous.

Man   Good for you.

Woman   Right. Okay, ready?

Man   I've been waiting for the last five minutes, this must be a war movie you've got in mind.

Woman   Now you're in the jungle and you are chopping up white people, start chopping.

Man   Wait, fuck, what do you mean?

Woman   What do I mean? You have never been to the movies on a Saturday morning? Come on, kid, I want at least a dozen different shots. Now look vicious and start chopping up white people in the jungle.

Man   This hole is not a jungle.

Woman   Who's the one that is acting all the time, now's your chance to prove yourself on camera, act as if you're in the jungle.

Man   What does these close-up shots have to do with the action?

Woman   Nothing, kid. All I want you to do is to pretend you're chopping up white people in some African jungle.

Man   I am not an African.

Woman   Alright, any bloody nationality.

Man   I am not taking any more photographs with any bloodclath chopper in my hand.

Woman   Why not for God's sake?

Man   Let bloodclath white people chop up bloodclath white people themselves.

Woman   What the hell are you talking about?

Man   I am talking about the effect of this kind of photo will have on Black people.

Woman   I don't understand.

Man   How can you, nobody does, and I don't think any fucker would care either except the innocent Blacks.

Woman   All I want is so photographs of you chopping up white people.

Man   Alright, bloodclath, bring the white man, bring him bloodclath here, let's do it for real rassclath, let's chop up the white man bloodclath.

Woman   Okay, kid, that is the spirit, keep it up.

Man   What are you talking about, I think I better put on my shirt.

Woman   What bloody for?

Man   Because I don't wanna take any more naked African photographs with any chopper in my hand.

Woman   Alright make it a naked Jamaican.

Man   I am not a savage.

Woman   Who said you were a savage?

Man   Well, that's what Black people would think if they see that kind of photograph of me.

Woman   So you're worried about people?

Man   If anyone from St Paul's see me like this they would think I have gone totally mad to rassclath.

Woman   What are you worried about? The only thing about St Paul's people is they're all poor.

Man   I don't care a bloodclath about St Paul's, I care about Black people.

Woman   Okay, okay. Let's cool down a bit. If you weren't so sensitive we could have had some good shots. It's silly really, really silly, stupid.

Man   And the first policeman from central police station who see the photograph would arrest me instantly.

Woman   Oh my God, are you frightened of the police too?

Man   Don't ask me foolishness.

Woman   Well, I think you are.

Man   You can think what you like. (*Picks up coffee-table book and looks at it.*) Is it true you have written a book?

Woman   No.

Man   But your name is on it.

Woman   I took the photographs.

Man   Did you make plenty of money?

Woman   No.

Man   White people never want to talk about money.

Woman   Oh I made thousands.

Man   That's a lot of money. What is the book about?

Woman   You can read it if you like.

Man   No.

Woman   You can have that copy.

Man   I expect someone write a book like this they make half a million. Are you gonna do any more books?

Woman   Yes I hope so.

Man   Are you gonna do one about Black people?

Woman   I might.

Man   Do one with lots of gambling and pretty chicks with plenty of money. It should do well amongst the Blacks when they make a movie of it.

Woman   Money and chicks.

Man   Are you gonna put me in it?

Woman   I might. Now tell me what makes you think you are a savage?

Man   I don't think I am a savage, did I say I was?

Woman   So why can't I take photographs of you holding the axe?

Man   Look, I want to better myself, I am a poet you know.

Woman   So you are not alone, there are lots of other poets.

Man   I am not stupid.

Woman   I didn't say you were but nevertheless you're acting as if you are.

Man   You know what I think?

Woman   Tell me what you think.

Man   Okay, okay. I will tell you.

Woman   Remember, all I wanted to do was to take some photos of you.

Man   I think somebody should have disturbed my mind when I was a child. How the bloodclath did I end up writing poetry?

Woman   You're still acting as if you you're a child.

Man   You're sculptor right?

Woman   That is correct.

Man   So why do you want to take photos of me?

Woman   So I can look at them.

Man   That I don't understand.

Woman   Why?

Man   Just forget about the photographs. Just make a statue of me and forget about the photos.

Woman   Look, I think all this fuss you are making is over nothing.

Man   Maybe.

Woman   I suppose you are right in some ways, complex.

Man   Complex, what's that?

Woman   Inferior complex.

Man   I am not inferior.

Woman   Are you really a poet?

Man   And a bloodclath gravedigger, the same way you are a photographer and a sculptor. I think you are going to sell those photographs.

Woman   So.

Man   So, I want some of the money.

Woman   Money eh, so that's what you want, well, you're not getting any.

Man   Why not?

Woman   It takes a long time to sell something.

Man   How long?

Woman   How long? Have you ever sold any of your poems?

Man   Nope.

Woman   So how do you expect me to sell a common everyday object like a photograph, just like that?

Man   Madam, the language in St Paul's is money.

Woman   Good for St Paul's.

Man   I think artists and artists should work together but white people and Black people is something else.

Woman   Black and white.

Man   That's politics.

Woman   Your politics is not my politics.

Man   Listen, I don't care if you take photos of me naked with two thousand spears in my hand.

Woman   You mean real African spears?

Man   Look, all my life I've been a guinea pig for white people and updated middle-class Blacks.

Woman   Oh I see, you're a lost soul.

Man   Can we talk artist to artist?

Woman   That's a mistake for start.

Man   Everybody makes mistakes, let's make a few ourselves.

Woman   You problem's money.

Man   Once again, yes.

Woman   Then you are not a bloody artist.

Man   Maybe I should have learnt my lesson at school.

Woman   Yes you should have and leave the problem of money to economists.

Man   I am living in St Paul's.

Woman   Who the fuck cares where you live. Jesus Christ, do you understand the suffering of the public at large?

Man   As far as I'm concerned the world starts and ends in St Paul's.

Woman   What the hell are you talking about?

Man   Lord God Almighty, when you're a Black artist and find yourself in the middle of St Paul's that is the end of life.

Woman   Stop taking the place so seriously.

Man   You have to. The place is always full of visitors from right-wing political group and left-wing Sunday churchgoers. St Paul's is one of the biggest excuses Bristol get for sending people to prison sensationally. Unfortunately for every reasonable person sensational prison sentence create further hate and so in turn you have everybody in St Paul's hating Bristol and the rest of society.

Woman   Listen, St Paul's is a first guinea pig for every crank and genius in the city.

Man   Bristol, eh, what a bloodclath place.

Woman   It's got a lot of England in it. Then the immigrants arrive in Bristol the petty crime rate shoots up. The truth is life in South Mead and Knowle can be just as painful.

Man   You talking to a Black man. He never leave St Paul's. It's Brixton, Chinatown, Moss Side.

Woman   You're on the wrong track. There's always a St Paul's in people's heads.

Man   What, St Paul's finally cracked me up as an artist?

Woman   You're not cracking up, there's a lot of artists worse off than you. It doesn't matter where you live. There's a problem everywhere for artists, except in the little square boxes they hold themselves.

Man   St Paul's is a box for me like a coffin.

Woman   Oh forget it – don't mention St Paul's – I'm tired of St Paul's – it's not the only place in England. Money and St Paul's and politics – it's stupid, stupid. You can't get stuck with all that.

Man   No fear, I left that place.

Woman   Well, okay then. You're alright. I know. You're a poet.

Man   The whole idea of life is to do something useful. I mean help people. Some of them are dying of starvation and diseases, how can a Black man be a poet in England while they are living in St Paul's?

Woman   The same way a woman has to be a sculptor in a hole like this.

Man   As far as I am concerned women are twice as wicked as men, if you was a man you wouldn't want to take naked pictures of me.

Woman   Ah, listen to his rubbish.

Man   Nobody understand what it's like for a Black poet who lives among white people and starving Black people.

Woman   Forget about white people or you'll never make any money from your writing. It is quite possible if you ever make any money from your poems you will lose your soul in the process.

Man   Sometimes I wonder what is the difference between a white rat and a black rat.

Woman   I suppose they help each other in their daily lives.

Man   All money have done for people so far is give them enough power to fool each other.

Woman   Pigs and rats have a lot in common.

Man   Do you believe in God?

Woman   Come on, kid, talk straight money, God's what's eating you.

Man   I wanna work.

Woman   Well, who's stopping you, the rats or the pigs?

Man   Oh my God. I feel so stupid, stupid. I might as well shoot myself, nobody don't bloody understand the fucking pain in my head. Why did I pick up a pen in the first place, make love not war, peace, perfect peace. Fuck politics, fuck them. One nation teach another to hate one another. I should have been a preacher, I could curse some of these bastards in Bristol face to face. The job these days is a gravedigger, digging grave for the young have a lot of future.

Woman   Are you worried about dying?

Man   I don't have the faintest idea.

Woman   I must admit you do interest me, I never met anyone like you.

Man   I find every human being a liar.

Woman   I understand that, you should be writing all the time.

Man   Who should I write for?

Woman   Yourself of course. I haven't had your experience but I like your madness, you should write for yourself.

Man   Not a bloodclath chance. I'm alright, Jack, I applied for a grave digger job last week at Brislington. I'm waiting for my interview. What a successful future.

Woman   That's not a bad job, maybe you'll find it easier writing epitaphs.

Man   A thousand epitaphs across the Atlantic Ocean.

Woman   Actually I'm very interested in your work.

Man   You don't know anything about my work.

Woman   Oh yes I do.

Man   Impossible. You don't understand. What I write. What I see in Bristol. All these people. The trees, the houses. All the faces. I am writing for the children and for the grandparents. For all the slaves that used to be here. I write for the future about now. Majority of population in Bristol, impossible they understand my work.

Woman   Why, I can understand.

Man   That's the nicest thing you have said to me today.

Woman   Don't let it go to your head.

Man   No it's not going to my head, it's going through my heart.

Woman   Don't worry, you'll live.

Man   What, you want me to do jump off the bridge? No, no, no! Stand there, look down the river.

Woman   Where my heart is, if you like. On the docks, right?

Man   You, you don't understand. You put me in the docks. You like all Bristol people – sooner see me in the dock getting prison sentence. Bristol is driving artist to the bottom of the sea. The sickness of these non-artist citizens in the island of Britain's practically rob the world of everything. You just the same.

Woman   Okay. Sorry, sorry.

Man   Right.

Woman   You like the sea?

Man   I love the sea. I going to set up home on the dock so I can look at sailors. I'm going to build a house on the water, surfing on the sea bed, write my poems in the water and drown all of Bristol with my words. Right.

Woman   I'll buy that.

Man   You can't buy poems at the bottom of the sea.

Woman   Can't make sculpture either. Read or write. You see this? (*Plan on wall.*)

Man   Yes, what is it?

Woman   It's what I want to do. You know that site by Grosvenor Road? I want to build this there sixty feet high. All timber.

Man   Like a bloody great tree-house.

Woman   Well, not quite – yes maybe it is . . .

Man   Well, do it! Get on and build it.

Woman   No chance. No one would let me put that there.

Man   Politics again see. Who the bloodclath . . .

Woman   A home at the mouth of Avonmouth, Bristol is not the only place where they fuck up artists' heads. Some help the government and the rest of the world's people to fuck up other artists. My sculptures, no way am I gonna sell any of my work, it must stand in the square for the poor to enjoy it. Nobody's gonna lock up my work in their castle-type houses. Sell books, yes, since most people never look at a book, lots of them can't even read or write.

Man   Who the bloodclath invented politics? Politics give some people bigger houses than others. Bigger houses create hate amongst smaller houses. The population are like rats who's afraid of a mouse. My body's in Bristol but my mind is at the mouth of the Avonmouth creeping about at the bottom of the sea. Bristol can have the Black body poet painting their bodies with their own blood, the fucking life of an artist is in the libraries with big iron gate. Come, one come all visit the best architectural building in the city, make your way through the iron gate enter the marbled floor hall, feel the warmth of the best central heating system ever created in modern America. Enjoy the life of our artist past and present stocked ten deep on our ancient shelves.

Woman   Modern American central heating, eh, I like that.

Man   Why did you become a sculptor?

Woman   I suppose I did like chopping down trees when I was a kid.

Man   A woodchopper, eh, fascinating – why didn't you chop down people instead?

Woman   Yes why didn't I, especially men?

Man   Well, I don't wish you to chop me down, although it would save me the trouble of digging other people's graves. Why should I bust my arse digging graves? Let the bodies stay on the streets so that everybody can smell the taste of death.

Woman   Have you change your mind already? A while ago you were looking forward to your adventurous gravedigging expedition.

Man   God Almighty, I feel stupid. I love Bristol but Bristol doesn't love me.

Woman   Come on, stop kidding yourself. Did you expect the white population of Bristol to love you?

Man   No not exactly but there's a lot of Black people living in Bristol.

Woman   Come on, what can the Blacks do to help you with your work?

Man   Most of them can stop trying to paint themselves white for a start.

Woman   That's a bit insulting to the Blacks isn't it?

Man   How can anyone insult the Blacks of Bristol with so much slave history in the past.

Woman   I should imagine that's quite easily done.

Man   Think again, madam, the Blacks cannot be insulted in Bristol.

Woman   I don't follow you.

Man   A nigger is a nigger.

Woman   Bloody hell, where's your blasted pride?

Man   I left it at the top Black Boy Hill and I should imagine yours is down White Ladies Road.

Woman   Fucking hell.

Man   Yes that is Bristol.

Woman   Ah stop it. Jesus Christ, what are you?

Man   A poet.

Woman   When are you gonna start building your house at the bottom of the sea?

Man   Soon.

Woman   Great.

Man   Are you pleased with me?

Woman   Yes, very.

Man   Well, it's love then.

Woman   From who to who?

Man   I will avoid that for the time being.

Woman   What are you working your way towards now?

Man   Loving you, some people have large mouth for the benefit of those who have quiet mouth. Quiet mouth complain about loud mouth because the quiet mouth thinks that by remaining quiet they are achieving their cup of tea with milk in it. Let's stop talking about other people's business and talk about love. I am getting on non-words answer from you. You are just giving me good old dirty looks. Still I could be lucky, I am sure if you are capable of chopping down trees when you were a child you should find me easy to cope with at the end of your chop-up.

Woman   Gonna go on working.

Man   How long have you lived in Bristol or were you born here?

Woman   Why do you want to know?

Man   Just trying to make conversation.

Woman   What have you been doing since we came in?

Man   Making conversation. Wondering why do you sentence yourself to slave labour for Bristol.

Woman   I work for myself.

Man   One bright morning about eight years ago I was walking across the Downs searching for bluebells. My heart was full with happiness so I look up to give thanks to God for another day. You know what? For the first time in England I see colours. In the sky and all around me there was colours, everywhere! Beautiful colours coming at me. A great sense of honesty take hold of me so I began to wonder about mankind. And why do they lay claims and god-colour that he gave to nature for themselves. And nobody not supposed to wear their colours unless you from them. I bought pen and paper that day and start writing poetry.

Woman   That's great. I like that. Better than politics.

Man   You know I was in politics.

Woman   Oh yes and we know how you got on.

Man   Right. I learned the ways of the Blacks.

Woman   What else did you learn?

Man   That I should give up writing and leave the Blacks to sort out their art works with the white man.

Woman   You're crazy.

Man   Does Black people interest you?

Woman   Maybe.

Man   I will tell you about the Blacks if you promise to tell me why Bristol cosmopolitan population is so wicked to each other.

Woman Funny, funny. I thought you knew. Why tell me your true feelings about the Blacks in Bristol?

Man I hate bloodclath middle-class Blacks from Barbados and Jamaica.

Woman I know that, who doesn't?

Man Bloodclath, even white people hate them and yet the only thing middle-class Blacks got in common with white people is that they like to be director of each other's lives and destinations. Have you ever been to bed with a Black man?

Woman Why, you fancy your chances do you?

Man I always fancy my chances.

Woman Since when?

Man You like sex?

Woman Sometimes. I am off men at the moment.

Man Good, then you fancy me?

Woman What makes you think that?

Man I am an artist. You must fancy me. Artists are different from other people.

Woman God above. What else is on your mind?

Man The whites of Bristol.

Woman What about the Blacks of Bristol?

Man Blacks of Bristol are fuckries, pure fuckries, fucked up by a few back-door dealing duck, fucking Blacks.

Woman That is not true.

Man What the bloodclath are you telling me?

Woman I am telling you to fall in love with your work and stop being so bitter about it all.

Man Alright I am falling in love with you instead. Jesus Christ, why for fuck's sake is middle-of-the-road Black people so stupid?

Woman You said that before.

Man I wish the white man would shoot them bloodclath kill every fucking one of the Black bastards who is keeping other niggers in starvation. Drive them bloodclath out of England. You know, I even went as far as to write a play about the Blacks in St Paul's.

Woman Oh really, that was good. What happened to it, did someone get it done for you?

Man It was called *No Soldiers in St Paul's*.

Woman   Where is it, what happened to it?

Man   The middle-class Blacks from Jamaica and Barbados get together with their good-class white friends and turn themselves into policeman and stop me from put it on in the streets of St Paul's.

Woman   Oh, how did they do that?

Man   I don't know, I'm not on the council.

Woman   You don't know what happened to your own play?

Man   No, my body break down before I could find out. I couldn't stop myself from vomiting, the sickness of their evil was upon me for months and months and I am still carrying the pain in my heart today. Sometimes I wonder in a dream for days if Black people will ever start taking care of each other.

Woman   That was cruel and vicious. Wicked bastards, they are all the same. Somehow we have to have the satisfaction of getting something together. The first thing you have to do is stop hating yourself. Start each day with love. I just got to keep working, I am sorry about your play.

Man   No don't worry, there's plenty more where that one's come from. I wonder if I could make everybody rich.

Woman   Or poor. No, that is no good, the problem is people's cruelty, not money.

Man   Jesus Christ in heaven. The world needs love, what is it to be Russia or America for a god?

Woman   Are you gonna write another play?

Man   No, all I want to do is talk foolishness all day.

Woman   Russia and America are two very large countries.

Man   Now I see it Russia and America is like Black people and white people. Russian is killing Russian for Russia.

Woman   And America is killing American for America. Good thinking.

Man   And politics is right in the middle, taking a beating.

Woman   Keep away from politics in England.

Man   Why?

Woman   Because you don't understand it.

Man   What, you must be joking. I understand that England and Ireland is at war.

Woman   I told you to keep out of English politics.

Man   What is politics in 1976?

Woman   A lot of nervous people.

Man   You have to go to university to understand politics and nobody stupid doesn't go to university.

Woman   Where did you learn that sort of shit?

Man   St Paul's.

Woman   Oh shut up.

Man   Temper, temper.

Woman   I'm going to cook, make some food. Want some beans, you want some?

Man   Yes, right – any beer?

Woman   How long have you lived in St Paul's?

Man   On and off for quite a few years. The Blacks, the Blacks, the best gravediggers. A hole in the road. Bring back hanging, live in a hole and leave your house around the corner.

Woman   Which planet are you on now?

Man   Planet Earth. I would like to drive a train to St Paul's.

Woman   I still don't understand about your play. What was the title of it again, 'No Soldiers in Heaven'?

Man   That's a good title but it was called *No Soldiers in St Paul's*. St Paul's a heaven for a lot of people's hidden hatred.

Woman   I was walking around the area the other day, there seems to be quite a lot of changes in the community.

Man   Were you inspecting the streets or the community?

Woman   Everything. It's changing, it is not like what it used to be. What happened to all the Blacks that used to live on Grosvenor Road?

Man   Gone shopping I suppose.

Woman   No seriously, where have they all got to?

Man   I am not sure, but a lot of them are now living in Easton.

Woman   Easton, eh. I wonder why? They should all go back to their own country.

Man   Why?

Woman   England is so overcrowded.

Man   I don't believe that for one minute.

Woman   Oh no?

Man   Are you thinking of running for parliament?

Woman   Why? You think immigration is the right policy for getting someone into parliament?

Man   That's dangerous talk.

Woman   Tell me, why did you say that the whole area of St Paul's is going to become a church? What a fantastic idea. Baptism every Sunday, getting everybody in church with the preacher man.

Man   And a preacher woman.

Woman   Deadly nightshade. (*Hands him the beer.*)

Man   Would you live in St Paul's?

Woman   I haven't thought about it.

Man   Well, you should.

Woman   What's that?

Man   I said you should think about living in St Paul's.

Woman   Why should you care where I live?

Man   I want to look after you.

Woman   I can look after myself and anyway you know fuck-all about St Paul's really. You seem to change your mind about St Paul's as fast as you can talk.

Man   I am only riding the waves and anyway the language in 1976 is survival.

Woman   Except person's survival is another man's death.

Man   Everybody talks about men's survival but nobody talks about women's survival.

Woman   That's politics again.

Man   Why are we keeping on over politics?

Woman   Oh hell, I don't know. I was born in the middle of it, can't escape.

Man   Oh yes you can.

Woman   How?

Man   Take up the Bible.

Woman   The Bible's a comedy.

Man   Well, what's wrong with comedy?

Woman   Nothing, except nobody laughs anymore.

Man   Are we having an argument about the Bible?

Woman   Hm, something like that.

Man   Who owns who?

Woman   Umm . . . that's a good note, work it out.

Man   I am stuck.

Woman   There is more to come. How are you gonna manage for oxygen when you build your house at the bottom of the sea?

Man   You are wrong to ask that question.

Woman   Why?

Man   Well, think about it.

Woman   I am thinking about it.

Man   Then don't you see that after I build my house at the bottom of the sea it will be too late to think about oxygen?

Woman   Ah, ah. Yes I see what you mean, you have to have oxygen or you wouldn't be able to build your house in the first place.

Man   Oh, girl, you are getting so clever.

Woman   Thank you.

Man   The easiest thing to do in the world is to fuck up another person's head.

Woman   So who is fucking up your head now?

Man   There's too much bad language going on between us.

Woman   I know. Very few people ever say what they should say.

Man   A genius in 1976 is one who can read between the lines.

Woman   And it shouldn't be like that. People make me so angry. I express myself by chopping down trees.

Man   You should be chopping off people's heads.

Woman   Yes, I know.

Man   Very good. You are getting cruel and mean so take up the Bible and show off the top of your panties, flash a leg past City Road.

Woman   How many years do you think it would take Black people in England to understand white people?

Man   Quite a few I should imagine and then again quite a few could be numberless.

Woman   How many grains of sand are on the seashore?

Man   Only the Bible could answer that one.

Woman   Or a comic strip.

Man   What are we doing with our lives?

Woman   Freaking out is helpful now and again. When are you gonna start writing again, man?

Man   The next full moon. We ask each other a lot of questions don't we?

Woman   Well, if anyone is listening they will learn not to ask so many questions.

Man   Can you concentrate on your work while I am talking rubbish?

Woman   Yes, this is nothing.

Man   What was this joint before it was your studio?

Woman   Guess.

Man   I can't, I never seen anything like it before.

Woman   Well, you won't believe me if I tell you.

Man   I have got no choice but to, try me.

Woman   Air-raid shelter, mad really? And it still is.

Man   Somehow I knew you was an atomic bomb. Bomb and wood can cause a lot of fireworks.

Woman   We could turn ourselves into human atomic bombs and start blasting from inside.

Man   Jesus, Jesus. What a bombshell, bombing your sculptures. And my poems will light the fuse.

Woman   We will scatter the ashes across the globe.

Man   Then we could be whatever we wanted, king, prostitute or warrior.

Woman   What would you be?

Man   A painter.

Woman   Painting Jesus across the fields.

Man   That's right. You would be the only man who would be strong enough to stay alive spiritually. I think God is a man and the devil is a woman.

Woman   Sure thing, buddy, who's God without the help of the devil?

Man   God and the devil will never part company.

Woman   Sure thing, kid. The devil and God live in the same house, they have never lost sight of each other.

Man   So carry on killing off each other people, because it is quite possible that God and the devil is man and wife.

Woman   Where do you think they live?

Man   In everybody's head. What a head trip.

Woman   Pain and more pain inside the rat race.

Man   The Bible is the only answer.

Woman   I am beginning to see this more clearly now and I don't like it one bit.

Man   Do you go to church?

Woman   When I was a child I used to.

Man   What are you now?

Woman   A fucking woman. Don't make me mad.

Man   Please don't, you will only add water to the brain.

Woman   You haven't got any brains.

Man   I have.

Woman   Where?

Man   In my bloodclath poems.

Woman   Where are your poems?

Man   In the first atomic bomb that goes off in St Paul's.

Woman   Funny bastard.

Man   You have gotta hurt people until you cripple them.

Woman   But that's a sin.

Man   That is all that is left of God, one's good world.

Woman   Then God and the devil have had a sex change.

Man   There's nothing illegal about that.

Woman   Come on, let's take some pictures.

Man   Okay, I'll be the cameraman.

Woman   Sure. I'll put on some music. (*Cassette.*)

Man   Bang, bang, one, two.

Woman   Ten, four.

Man   Capitalist.

Woman   Slavery.

Man   Concrete.

Woman   Jungle.

Man   Desert.

Woman   The army.

Man   Queen Victoria.

Woman   Generals.

Man   Queen Victoria.

Woman   Bristol.

Man   White Ladies Road.

Woman   Chains.

Man   Sex.

Woman   Love.

Man   Sure.

Woman   The world.

Man   Love.

Woman   Human.

Man   Pigs.

Woman   Rats.

Man   Children.

Woman   White.

Man   Black, white and fucking Blacks.

Woman   Stop.

Man   Sure, baby, sure.

Woman   Are you getting some good shots?

Man   Sure, baby, sure. They are all in my head.

Woman   Sure, baby, sure.

Man   The have-nots are leaving the woods.

Woman   You don't put cider in the fridge.

Man   Captain bleak weather was reading the weather report this morning.

Woman   Let's dance.

Man   For who?

Woman   For music.

Man   Music, eh, that's interesting.

Woman   Nobody understands.

Man   They have to.

Woman   Sure, baby, sure. The Bible, that's a good one.

Man   The most important thing in England is heat.

Woman   The starting of the heatwave.

Man   The sun shines everywhere.

Woman   That's true.

Man   Except in an air-raid shelter.

Woman   You could fool me.

Man   It's your turn next.

Woman   Time passes.

Man   Blame the atomic bomb.

Woman   Shell shock.

Man   You lost me.

Woman   No I haven't.

Man   I wanna talk about love.

Woman   I know, I wanna talk about love too.

Man   It's a difficult subject.

Woman   People's moods change very quickly.

Man   Jesus Christ, I hate politics.

Woman   Well, if you can't beat them, join them.

Man   Actually, let's talk about this seriously.

Woman   Sure, go ahead.

Man   Bristol's a city and county.

Woman   Not for a few years now.

Man   Yes, I forget.

Woman   I told you, you don't know anything about England.

Man   Well, I think that when all the different political groups in Great Britain amalgamated themselves then they will end up with left wing on one side.

Woman   And right on the other.

Man   Right, so you'll end up with a bird.

Woman   That makes good sense, birds do have a left wing and a right wing.

Man   It doesn't make sense.

Woman   What does? The only thing that makes sense is that people should stop killing each other off.

Man   You need a lot of love to stop the killing and right now the world is very short of that and it's getting worse every winter, but why?

Woman   Don't ask me.

Man   Right, I got it. The next general election nobody should vote.

Woman   Then what?

Man   I don't know.

Woman   Try again.

Man   Yes, I know everybody would stop and think for that day.

Woman   They would have to.

Man   I am glad I came into your air raid shelter, the hate on the street would surely kill me.

Woman   Yes, I know what you mean. When you walk the streets you can almost see the heat in the people, penetrating your bowels, you listen to some of the shit, it makes you vomit.

Man   And when you think that the bad grown-ups was once good babies.

Woman   Some of them was pretty little babies, where did it all go wrong?

Man   Well, at least we are getting to know each other. Black people are getting inside my thinking again.

Woman   It's your play and what they done to it, isn't it?

Man   Yes. Sometimes they make me go out and look for white people to apologise for them, for begging them to give Black people enough space to breathe free oxygen. You know something, I don't give a fuck, I am gonna spend the rest of my life teaching people to love each other. Fuck it, I don't care if it kills me.

Woman   I will go along with you on that one. That's a good note.

Man   You mean that do you?

Woman   Yes I do.

Man   Thank you. I'm sure you're a kind person.

Woman   Yes, fuck the hate between Russia and America, I am tired of it all.

Man   And the English is naive about it.

Woman   Yes they are.

Man   What's the first thing you think we should do together?

Woman   Stop and think together.

Man   I don't hate anybody individually, I just hate what they do to other people's lives.

Woman   It's gonna be hard work but we'll do what we set out to do.

Man   And if we don't start soon we will never leave the air raid shelter.

Woman   Yes, we are not alone in thinking but most of the time people are afraid to show their true love. When we leave the air raid shelter let's kick off by going to church.

Man   At least we will be able to meditate.

Woman   There is a God you know.

Man   Maybe he's a ponce.

Woman   Yes, it's quite possible he could be poncing off all the devil's disciples.

Man   Then, he's a good ponce.

Woman   Good for him but bad for the devil's disciples.

Man   The next time I do any writing I'm gonna write about God and the devils of Devil's Dyke.

Woman   You should also paint a picture to go with it. We can't lose, we are both human guinea pigs inside the rat race.

Man   You can't run a country without a government can you?

Woman   No you can't.

Man   What is the government? May I ask the same question I've been asking for years?

Woman   Public hanging.

Man   Jail the bastard. Hang the bastards, the government said so.

Woman   We can't go on like this for much longer.

Man   But really and truly not many things make sense in this modern society.

Woman   Yes, art and artists into shit street.

Man   Wake up you sinners and listen.

Woman   I wanna spend most of my time talking to people, helping them, teaching them. I have done nothing for the last six months except to run away from the head-trip people of Bristol. Please God let the sun shine tomorrow. Love and hate are sister and brother. Fuck it I am gonna take my work to the people myself.

Man   I piss and shit all over my work, they make good fertiliser for the next set of green grass at home.

Woman   Where is home?

Man   Anywhere my head is.

Woman   That's nice.

Man   I got the blues on a Monday morning train. Sunday morning blues is Friday's pay packet, yours sincerely blues is fading. Dark night, street dreaming.

Woman   Are you a dreamer?

Man   Dreaming blues.

Woman   What have we done today?

Man   Complain about our blues.

Woman   With the help of a few cigarettes.

Man   That's nice, yes.

Woman   Yes, that's nice, we must keep on going kid.

Man   Every time a person use the word friend or love they should be proud of themselves.

Woman   That's a nice thing to say.

Man   A friend to love is good for the heart of the innocence.

Woman   And that is the truth about nothing.

Man   Yes, it is true but nothing can remain forever.

Woman   You know those bastards who stop you from putting on your play for the benefit of the poor Blacks in St Paul's so that the Clifton people could see what they are doing to those poor Blacks? Fucking hell, it's a good job I didn't know you then or together we'd get hold of one of those big artillery guns that the army have on the street in Belfast and blow their fucking heads off, to pieces, one by one.

Man   Man to women.

Woman   Woman to man. Man, you understand that to love someone is to give them back their freedom before it was taken away from them. You cannot categorise freedom. Words can be a great asset to a person but love is in the air rushing around all the time waiting like oxygen that become breeze blowing for the trees. Love's greatest friend is living things, the real thing, the real living, unseen thing. It's a woman's choice to choose colours. I like to see rainbows in other people's eyes. Your eye silently, peacefully, carefully. And it is a never-ending pastime for me. I have a warm feeling coming on in my belly.

Man   Well, inside of me is twisted and painful as if I don't know any words for my next sentence, but something else inside me driving me beyond where my mind have never been. Therefore, at this moment, I cannot co-ordinate with other planets why the bloodclath this have to happen to me in an air raid shelter.

Woman   Good, you have too much mouth for your size.

Man   Jesus Christ, what are you doing to me?

Woman   I am telling you to watch it and not too much sweet words.

Man   I want to go to bed.

Woman   Get on with your work in your head and don't bother with too many words. Here is a paintbrush, you can use my pen if you'd rather start writing your Devil's Dyke play.

Man   Woman, don't think for one minute you can burn me out.

Woman   I was waiting for you but you didn't know that.

Man   Jesus Christ, what have I done?

Woman   Nothing except to cross Black people and moan about Bristol. Bristol is good to you. You are lucky and don't know it.

Man   What the bloodcloth are you talking about Bristol being good to me. How can a person live in St Paul's and be lucky?

Woman   You're getting ready to start talking about money again and ready to give it all up, lazy bastard. How are you going to help anyone if you just sit here doing nothing?

Man   I don't want anything.

Woman   What did you expect to get?

Man   Some kind of sympathy.

Woman   You think you know me well enough to ask for my sympathy?

Man   I didn't have to think.

Woman   Yes I know.

Man   Why are you attacking me?

Woman   Listen it's important for a person to do his work properly.

Man   The strength of a person's head is to sit silently and listen to other people's shit.

Woman   You think I am talking shit do you?

Man   I wonder if we're normal to rassclath?

Woman   Half the shit you talk, if you spent ten minutes a day to put it on paper maybe some sense would come out of you, you don't know what you want, do you?

Man   You don't know what it is like, do you? Why if you love someone you can only say dirty things about them once? Again my mind and thinking is packing up on me. I am getting funny. If only I could make every single person hate me then I might my find myself somewhere else in another planet. I should have left other people's business alone, but you cannot kill yourself before you are dead. Life must go on even if you make one million mistakes per second you must stand in the middle of the road and feel the shame of nakedness, even if you are not a streaker. Under no circumstances should you give up. Let the mind roll, let it roll. Madness take over from the little sanity that left inside of you, still in your mind's head there is vacancy for everything that goes on in the bottom of the mind. The wind in my throat is developing into a hurricane, lungs are saying I cannot take the pressure. Yes, yes, it is true love exist. Yes, it is true and when it happens to you your mind is turning like lightning, flashing across the sky in bright sunlight, your subconscious mind can't believe what your subconscious mind is substituting, fantasy and reality it is all happening to me in an air raid shelter. Everything is catching up with me. Shame and ecstasy is driving more and more into insanity. No time to answer, words cannot come, so I will begin what I don't want to say. I am sorry, Lord, forgive me for what I have done. Fuck the church, sorry, padre. I am looking at the object, the thing, the woman, I am a man. It's been all my life, she's here. We have both create a third person, the unborn child exist. I am weak, standing or sitting, the happiness that is to come, fifty years ahead. I am waiting in my head. Are you thinking what is going on, what were you doing all your life? Somebody's laughing, I don't care, since nobody is laughing, it's all in the mind's eye. Seeing things in your head, fate and strength is deep in you, gone, gone my heart become my head, beating the bass drum, saying I love you, I love you. What are you doing? You don't know. If you have ever known anything, the thinking is good, so it pains, it hurts. When last time you was a child? I love you woman. I am gonna spend the rest of my life working for you. You are not asking me questions, but I have all the answers, yes, yes, to everything. I get it back, nothing matters anymore, yesterday words is today emotions, burning, burning me up. You are strong into the future, so don't hustle me because from now on business to look after each other. A peaceful life to each other is what we wanted all our life, so I am going to holla and scream, because it never happen to either of us before. So, woman, shake and tremble with the volcano that is coming on. I am not fucking lazy. I've walked the street of the island of Great Britain with the greatest heavyweight unseen load on my back for you. Ten thousand soldiers emotions run freely in my veins, with enough power, with blood and sweat. I am asking to touch you, for other dimensions to come in our lives. The love for you is happening right here and now. The love for a woman is what I have been looking for all my life. Bloodclath, I am alive and well with passion and desire for you.

Woman   I will go all the way with you at that level, but nothing less not one bloody inch. Never drop below par or we will both die. I can feel what you are saying, it's real to me, to life, to us but don't ever come searching for sympathy from me.

Man   I don't want any sympathy.

Woman   Bloody hell, bent and glory, you are not gonna get any. What do you think I've been doing all my life, waiting to give you sympathy?

Man   I don't know, I didn't ask.

Woman   Just make sure you keep it that way, I don't want any tired, emotional, lazy sympathiser hanging around my neck.

Man   I am not lazy.

Woman   Well, why aren't you working? You must work, get it all out of your head.

Man   You mean we, don't you?

Woman   Yes I do.

Man   You look beautiful when you're angry.

Woman   Thank you.

Man   Still, I must say I feel better. I didn't know I got it in me, I get it all out didn't I?

Woman   Okay. Let's give it a try, right? Give it a try, right? What next? Get the hammer and chisel.

Man   Where are they?

Woman   Over there somewhere, find it.

Man   Right, what do you want me to do?

Woman   Work, what else? We're gonna work on this piece together, we will do something right and proper.

Man   What are we gonna do right and proper with this piece of wood?

Woman   We're gonna cut a double album.

Man   Yes, I like music.

Woman   Good.

Man   Thank you.

Woman   This is music in the wood.

Adventure Inside Thirteen

Characters

Vince
Dal
Roach
Merchant
Wyvern
Bell
Reitha
Helen
Cutter

Act One

Darkness. Music of Stevie Wonder singing 'Big Brother'.

Lights. Morning. Adventure playground.

Enter **Vince**. *Goes to locker in shed. Looks for his tool-kit. Takes out electric drill, hammer, screwdriver, etc., comes to tobacco tin. Rolls cigarette, lights it.*

Vince (*listening*)   We live in a house the size of a matchbox.

Fade down music and lights.

Lights.

Dal   Hello, world. This world is upside down today. It's a big big world.

Vince   You were quite busy yesterday.

Dal   You're telling me.

Vince   I had a bellyful of it myself.

Dal   You didn't come home last night.

Vince   No, I was at the hostel.

Dal   What? Again and all night?

Vince   Yes and I didn't sleep either.

Dal   How could you?

Vince   They were at it again.

Dal   Never-ending and on and on it goes. If you were living in New York, you would be way up the Peace Corps ladder. No, no I mean that.

Vince   I know what you mean. How was the meeting?

Dal   Bus fares is probably going up again.

Vince   What? When?

Dal   Two weeks.

Vince   They can't do that.

Dal   They have done it.

Vince   What about the playground? Did they like our policy.

Dal   They didn't have time to discuss Adventure Thirteen.

Vince   You mean they didn't even talk about our application?

Dal   No, there was almost a riot amongst the councillors. I sat there for half an hour, thinking they were having their annual competition.

Vince   Bus fares went up only months ago.

Dal   The council meeting was a gas. Some of the councillors were very angry.

Vince   How can the poor survive in this bureaucratic society?

Dal   Is that a question?

Vince   Bloody hell, they are cutting back on education and putting up the bus fares at the same time. Where is the justice?

Dal   I feel like singing the blues. How bad was it at the hostel?

Vince   Very bad. Some West Indians don't like other West Indians.

Dal   Oh I see. Is that what started the trouble this time? Was Merchant in action?

Vince   Yes, but he couldn't do anything to help the tension. Wyvern was arguing with him.

Dal   How do they manage to live together in the same flat? They never stop cutting each other's throat.

Vince   I think they know exactly what they are doing.

Dal   Do you mean cutting each other's throat?

Vince   They are not so stupid as they would have us believe.

Dal   Helen knows what they are doing.

Vince   Yes, but for how long?

Dal   She knows where it's at.

Vince   That is because she is a woman.

Dal   The council meeting was a natural excitement for me. My first one in Great Britain.

Vince   Was Helen with you?

Dal   No, just Reitha and myself.

Vince   Is she coming in today?

Dal   Yes I suppose so.

Vince   Is she coming in today?

Dal   Pardon me.

Vince   Is Reitha coming to the adventure playground?

Dal   She said she was. We had a drink with Roach last night. That meeting was just something else. We didn't get home until early morning. We were sure you was in bed. Reitha was very excited about you. She is secretive isn't she? You love her don't you?

Vince   I don't know what love is, we get along all right.

Dal   She said she was going to see Bell sometime this morning.

Vince   So she won't be here before later afternoon. That's if she turns up.

Dal   She will turn up.

Vince   Where the hell is Roach?

Dal   We had a drink with him last night. I said that before didn't I, Vince?

Vince   When did you have a drink with Roach?

Dal   After the meeting. Are you listening to me?

Vince   He said he was going to be early today.

Dal   Well, he was drunk last night.

Vince   He will never make it here today, I know it.

Dal   Yes he will.

Vince   Not if he was drunk last night.

Dal   He's worried about his job.

Vince   What have he got to worry about. He's got more money than me.

Dal   You like the Blacks don't you? I'm not saying that because you are going out with Reitha.

Vince   We are not going out. We are living together.

Dal   That's what I mean.

Vince   Reitha is a person.

Dal   She's a Black woman.

Vince   What does it matter if she is Black or white?

Dal   Or a man or a woman? But the fact remains she is a Black woman, sweetheart. I like her, she's a sister.

Vince   Did Roach say what time he would be here?

Dal   Yes, early. Everybody will be here today. Cutter is coming too.

Vince   What for? I can't stand the pigs. Fucking pigs.

Dal   He came yesterday after you left with Reitha.

Vince   I can't stand the fucking pigs.

Dal   He's on the committee.

Vince   And don't I know it. He's got the biggest mouth. He's for the National Front.

Dal   He's a policeman.

Vince   He's more than a policeman.

Dal   He's got brains.

Vince   He's good isn't he? None of the Blacks knows he's a policeman.

Dal   Except Merchant and Wyvern.

Vince   I don't mean them.

Dal   They are both Black. I just want to sing the blues. Here comes Helen with Reitha and Bell. She's wearing pink. Jesus Lord, she's wearing pink. I don't believe it, she's wearing a pink dress. What the hell is she up to? Why did she choose that dress? My God, I say she's funny woman indeed. I hope she don't wear pink at the next committee meeting. She's chatting with Bell and Reitha. Both of them are looking at her dress. What a day this is going to be. Helen is in pink.

Vince   I won't be here when the pig turn up. Bus fares is going up again. Where is their logic? When Roach gets here, tell him I'm looking at the slope. Anyway nothing can stop us now. If the council continue to turn us down we will go somewhere else.

Dal   I can imagine how hard you and your committed have worked in the past to make this project so successful as it stands today.

Vince   I am off to look at the slope.

Dal   What about Reitha?

Vince   What about her?

Dal   Talk to her. Tell her where you spent the night.

Vince   What is the matter with you?

Dal   Nothing. Except that she would like to see you now that she is here.

Vince   I am not running away.

Dal   Wait, here comes Roach.

Vince   Where is he?

Dal   He's here.

Vince   Good.

Dal   Hi, Roach. What goes with the machine?

Roach   It's a tape recorder. I have been thinking. I'm a bit shaken about the council meeting last night. So I have decided if any of the kids turn up outside the gate, I would like to interview them. You know, see what they think.

Dal   That's a good idea.

Roach   So, Vince, while you was at the hostel last night something else was going on at the council meeting.

Vince   Yes so I heard. But they can't stop us. Like fuck they can.

Roach   Yes, Vince, I will hand it to you. You have worked very hard for the adventure playground. It's a real Adventure Inside Thirteen for me since we take over from Joseph.

Vince   Yes I have had a lot of help from a number of dedicated people. There is nothing wrong with this neighbourhood. It's the council that is fucking it up. By doing nothing about the NF. My grandfather was a coalminer. My father grew up in shit. We never had anything. Not even a toy when I was a child. His father could not afford to buy himself shoes in some of the coldest winters. But my father work hard enough until he buy his own boots.

Dal   It was a sad night for us at the council meeting.

Roach   You mean last night performance? What I can't understand is the amount of hard work and excitement that was going on before the council meeting. I tell you the truth, the council fool me too. I believe we would have got a direct grant from them. I was preparing myself for a big celebration today. Instead I had to get drunk last night. Yes I was pissed out of my head. Vince, are we going to work on the slope?

Vince   Yes, when you're ready.

Roach   What do you think about the tape recorder?

Vince   Yes it is a good idea to know what the kids think. That's if they come anywhere near the playground.

Dal   You mean because of last night at the hostel? But that's been going on and off now for days.

Vince   And with the fear that the National Front is going to pay us a visit is not helping the situation one bit.

Roach   Well, I aim to get the kids' voice on tape. And their signature on paper.

Dal   What's your next move, Vince?

Vince   I don't know. I will listen to what the others have to say then I will decide.

Dal   Reitha seems to think we should organise a demonstration. I am sure that is what the three of them are discussing together.

Roach   What happened to Helen trouser suit?

Dal   She have changed. She is a brand new woman.

Roach   Merchant say Helen is the first woman he ever see in a trouser suit.

Dal   She looks lovely in her pink dress.

Roach   Was Merchant at the council meeting?

Vince   No he was at the hostel.

Roach   That's right. How bad was it really, Vince?

Dal   Vince didn't come home last night.

Roach   What was you at the hostel all night?

Vince   Except for a few hours at Merchant and Wyvern pad.

Roach   Well, weren't they with you at the hostel?

Vince   Yes but the pigs throw them out.

Dal   What, the cops throw Merchant out of the hostel? The CRC is not going to like that.

Roach   Tell us more, Vince.

Vince   Merchant and Wyvern were shouting at each other. There was a lot of pigs all over the building. I was glad to get away from the pigs. So I went back with Merchant and Wyvern.

Roach   Well, did they have a punch-up?

Vince   You mean the pigs and the kids?

Roach   No, Merchant and Wyvern.

Vince   No.

Dal   They will never fight each other except with guns. I am going to check out the girls and see what they are doing.

Roach   Well it was seven of us that cracked the barrier and stigma that surrounded the figure thirteen. Seven is close to heaven. Since Cutter and Dal joined us we have become a massive nine. The figure nine is something to astonish every human being. Nine and nine is eighteen. Eight and one is nine. Three nines is twenty-seven. Seven and two is nine. And so it goes all the way up to the hundred per cent mark. The figure nine will always come back at you. It is a power to the nine of us for shaping and making Adventure Inside Thirteen. The hostel is in a bad state since we closed the playground. The future of all playgrounds look shaky to me. We need more action.

Vince   Don't put too much faith in Cutter and Dal.

Roach   Wyvern and Merchant should let the kids solve some of their own problems. Merchant wants the CRC to take over the hostel. Merchant thinks the CRC team can deal quite adequately with the hostel problem. And not having the pigs there every time there is any trouble. Merchant to link up the playground and the hostel with the CRC. Wyvern thinks the CRC is worse than the pigs. I can't stand the pigs. I am glad both of them hate the pigs.

Vince   So that's what's going on in the kids' heads. The fight is between Merchant and Wyvern. I wonder which one of them is going to win the kids' support. Wyvern would like a closer tie with the hostel and this project and keep the CRC away from the hostel and the playgrounds.

Roach   Merchant will never accept that.

Vince   No he is a true CRC man. We're going to discuss it at the next meeting but the both of them was clashing at hostel all day yesterday. They were trying to find out what the kids think about it all and whole situation blew up late last night.

Roach   Did the cops take any of the kids in?

Vince   No but they punch a few.

Roach   They wouldn't do much with you there.

Vince   No, man, those pigs hates me.

Roach   So that's what Merchant is up to. I think he wants to be a councillor.

Vince   He could do well as a liberal.

Roach   Would you support him or is that kind of politics too light for you?

Vince   I don't know, man. I am pretty pissed off at the moment. It could be interesting if we ever had a Black councillor in the neighbourhood.

Roach   I agree with you. But I am not sure if Merchant is the right person.

Vince   Here they come.

Roach   That's right, Merchant and Wyvern in person.

Merchant   It is not a question of who's running what. My interest remains top priority for our Black youth.

Wyvern   It will never work with your attitude towards the kids.

Merchant   Hello, Vince, Roach.

Roach   Yeah.

Vince   Hi, Wyvern.

Merchant   We have to look at the whole future problems of the Black youth in this neighbourhood.

Vince   What do you think, Wyvern?

Wyvern   You mean the problem of the Black youth in this particular neighbourhood?

Vince   Yes.

Wyvern   I haven't changed.

Merchant   Go on, explain your policy. Put you plan on the table.

Wyvern   I am warning you to stop treating me like a white man. What are you trying to do? Make every Tom, Dick and Harry a decent citizen in the district? You are not the make of man, Merchant, you are only one of them. The CRC made a bad choice when they chose you to work for their organisation. Maybe that's why I refuse to go anywhere near the building. You are getting more than three thousand a year from the government. What for?

Merchant   Put your policy on the table.

Roach   Merchant, what you think of the council meeting last night? They didn't even discuss our application.

Merchant   That is only a small setback. But nevertheless disappointing. The council have no choice but to discuss our project in the near future. And with no doubt favourable in our interests. The CRC is the middle road of the government. We at the CRC is not too late to gather the lost sheep. What we want is every man hand on that table. A total togetherness in a policy that will bring virtue to the committee. A policy that care for every individual with no turning back to the old days. A solid foundation to forge ahead on a respectable future. There is no rejoicement between the police and the Black youth of our time. I see a vast gap between them. We must bridge that gap and common sense is the only way out. We must deal with the problem as we see fit and don't leave a single youth lagging behind. The CRC can easily deal with every Black youths' problem. We are growing every day. We are not the government. We are just part of the government. We have our problem at the CRC. Some of them extremely frustrating. But nevertheless more satisfying results than any other part of the government that is dealing with Black youths problems of today. When I choose to live with poor man on the streets, I will know where to go to argue for his or her rights. We must not just think of the youth of today, we must also think of the youth of tomorrow. We must rid out streets of its dirty name. No dirt, clean all the streets in the neighbourhood. Let every citizen have a hand in the everyday running of their environment. Our kids have nowhere to go. No holds barred in every man's prosperity. The tactics of some of these youths are deplorable. The future is the only way out. The future I personally referred to is that every man gets a bite of the apple. Some of the youths are not going along others. We must find out why. And for God sake when we do, let's do something about it. We must get the youths to participate in their own future good and a solid standing ovation for the man or the youth who can by the sweat of his brow. His daily contribution must count towards the good of the local committee. I will not fall asleep and let things rot under my feet. I am no uncle Tom, never was and never will be. No tree can survive without its original roots. A good tree needs its root firmly embedded in the earth. Let's look at all the problems carefully that exist between the CRC, the hostel and the adventure playground. If we could link the three of them together surely we would be a stronger committee? Hence we would be more positive in our future role for the neighbourhood. I must confess that I am dismal and blatant for the future of the hostel. There was no need for such madness last night. They are giving the police an open invitation to visit the hostel. I want to keep the police away from the hostel. Let we the senior citizens of the local committee solve their problems. We know our youths best not the police.

Vince   Let's go and have a look at the slope, Roach.

Roach   Sure, Vince. You must make that speech again, Merchant. I would like to tape it. Your head is really turning over. Boy, oh boy. See you in a while, Wyvern.

Wyvern   Yes later.

Merchant   Are you staying in tonight?

Wyvern   Is it important?

Merchant   Yes and no.

Wyvern   Well, it is yes and no if I go out or stay in.

Merchant   Oh, well, please yourself.

Wyvern   Have I done anything else?

Merchant   I am better at sarcasm than you. Look, I am tired. It is very hard at the office. Somebody somewhere while we was at the hostel yesterday, somebody stabbed Joseph in the park, Wyvern.

Wyvern   That's right, I heard something about it.

Merchant   Who done it?

Wyvern   Who done what?

Merchant   Who stabbed Joseph?

Wyvern   He is a white man isn't he?

Merchant   Jesus Lord God be merciful. Does it matter whether he is white or Black?

Wyvern   But he's not Black.

Merchant   How did you know that Joseph got stabbed in the park?

Wyvern   How did you know?

Merchant   Never you mind. He's one of the best playground workers that we ever had in the neighbourhood. He works very hard on this project before Vince took over.

Wyvern   You mean he was a good policeman.

Merchant   He works for a full year with those Black kids in the hostel for nothing.

Wyvern   That was kind of him. Was he writing a book for the cause?

Merchant   Who stab him?

Wyvern   How the hell should I know?

Merchant   You are the one who spend all day with them in the coffee bars.

Wyvern   So that's the way your mind works. The white man get stabbed in the park and you immediately think it is some Black youths. And you even went as far as saying that he was my friend.

Merchant   I tell you, boy, if it is one of your friends that stabbed Joseph they have had it. The police is combing the whole vicinity with a fine-tooth comb.

Wyvern   That's it, I am staying indoors tonight.

Merchant   You can't, I'm having a meeting in the front room.

Wyvern   I am not going out. If I go out the pigs will only question me.

Merchant   You little nincompoop, you Jacobin. You find it fit and proper to address the British police as pigs.

Wyvern   What's the matter with you, you stupid cunt. Everybody call the police pigs.

Merchant   No blood likely. Not me, boy. I never have or ever will call the British police pigs. I myself have had a lot of trouble with the police in the past. I am no new horse to the mill.

Wyvern   And yet you don't even worth the weight off a fucking donkey.

Merchant   We the older generation have nothing in common with you younger coffee-bar freaks. Why do you think we are applying for urban aid. To support murderers? Flippin' hell, a man like Joseph done nothing else but help young Blacks since he left university.

Wyvern   Maybe he wants to be Jesus father.

Merchant   Fuck off, bastard. I might damage my career if you stay at home tonight.

Wyvern   What home? You mean the hell house we share together?

Mercant   That's it. You must find you own heaven.

Wyvern   I will soon as you go to that government office and don't come back.

Merchant   That was not nice. I am responsible citizen. I have done a lot for Black people. I demand some respect from you and your coffee-bar criminals.

Bell   Well said, Mr Merchant. You speaking proper words of wisdom.

Cutter   Hi, Vince.

Vince   Hi, Cutter. I suppose you all heard the news of last night council meeting?

Cutter   Yes we have.

Reitha   He didn't come home last night.

Roach   That's right he was at the hostel all night. Lord Jesus, Wyvern, you still sitting down under Merchant pressure.

Wyvern   Yes, man.

Dal   It's a nice gathering right on time.

Cutter   So, Wyvern, there was trouble in the hostel?

Vince   Yes and there was a stabbing in the park. We were right to close the adventure playground.

Bell   Merchant, how is life at the office?

Merchant   Rough but I am still bearing up.

Wyvern   Cutter is always interested in the trouble in the vicinity.

Roach   I know and with lots of details.

Reitha   Vince, I am sorry about the council meeting last night.

Helen   The council meeting was a shambles.

Dal   So how goes it, Cutter?

Cutter   Fine, fine.

Bell   Merchant, when am I going to see?

Merchant   Soon, Bell, very soon.

Roach   Wyvern, I have my tape recorder with me here. I want to talk to the kids if they turn up outside the gates.

Wyvern   Man, we had bad trouble at the hostel last night. They may not turn up.

Vince   I am off to the SS.

Reitha   I will come with you.

Dal   Cigarette, Cutter?

Cutter   Yes, I'll have one. I drop by your place last night. But you wasn't in.

Dal   No, we were at the council meeting. It was a gas.

Helen   The meeting was a shambles. From the report I have had and some of them from quite reliable sources.

Vince   Bye, everybody.

Reitha   Bye, Helen.

Helen   Bye, I will expect you at seven.

Roach   What about the slope?

Vince   Leave it. We'll have a bash at it later. I'll probably go to sleep after I've left the SS.

Wyvern   Yes, Vince, you look worn out. Try and get some sleep.

Dal   No supper for you tonight, Reitha.

Reitha   No, I am eating with Helen.

Cutter   I will eat her portion.

Dal   Okay, eight o'clock.

Helen   We will never get a council grant at this rate.

Vnce   Later.

Reitha   Ciao, everybody.

Merchant   I must get some sleep myself.

Roach   Merchant, you're as strong as a mule. You don't need no sleep. I must pay you and Wyvern a visit in the near future.

Wyvern   That's all right. As long as you don't bring the tape recorder with you.

Roach   You frighten I will tape you and Merchant secrets?

Merchant   There is no secret whatsoever that existed between me and Wyvern.

Bell   Helen, you must keep those councillors. We must get that grant.

Helen   Oh I will.

Bell   What do you think we should do about the council meeting last night?

Helen   It was a disgrace. They didn't even debate our application.

Merchant   Well, the council set-up is a funny one. Well, you never know. Perhaps this is only a small setback. We must gather more power around us. Straighten out the right people from the wrong people. A natural civilisation need natural people. No false prophet. If I was to put my history on table, it would be one with a complete knowledge of the whole neighbourhood. The councillors are only teasing us. They are waiting on us to come up with a fair and clear-cut decision. We must look deeper into our whole policy for the adventure playground. The people is our customer. We must serve them properly. Our Black youths will have no future. We must also root out the evil ones. Our Black youth must not have a future of prison sentences like their fathers. The Black youths of today find themselves in the middle of an intellectual war. Therefore we must make our point again to the council. I myself have dealing with more than a dozen councillors. A great majority of them are my personal friends. We must move with the time. We must make ourselves stronger. And more positive in all respects. A storm may be gathering around us. Nothing can stop the positiveness of the CRC in this project. The Black youths of today must be our main interest. Surely there is enough brutality around us to convince us of the facts. But first we must come together for Adventure Inside Thirteen to have a successful future. If nine of us are strong enough to take the figure thirteen and make it so positively as it is today, that to me is the most crucial element that exists for the benefit of the Black youth. There will always be active progressing role of co-operation between the CRC and this project Adventure Inside Thirteen.

Helen   I am well out of it. And very disgusted with the whole bloody mess we have here. There is not enough money in the kitty of Adventure Inside Thirteen to keep it turning over for another month. Vince has voluntarily relinquished his salary. He has showed us the way ahead. But this project is not going ahead, the council has stopped it. We must pull our socks up and convince the council that if they don't support Adventure Inside Thirteen, there will be unforeseeable damage done to the neighbourhood which is already having a diminishing relationship with the council. Dal has joined us recently and already has added a solid force of vitality to the cause. And I have never seen a more stronger, courageous young woman in this area. The council meeting was a sham and it distresses me. We must look somewhere else for our money and we must re-open the playground as soon as possible. Roach, how is the new slope coming along?

Roach   We will finish in a week or less.

Helen   There is enough strength in us to move a mountain. I say we should not just sit and wait for a decision from those silly little men that run our council offices. There are several trusts and associations which will be quite happy to give us some money. I would like to see Dal get paid a proper salary. There is a place for her here and we need her.

Bell   I would like to remove this project and put it right inside the council house. Let's show them that we mean to clean up the neighbourhood and make it a proper place for our youngsters. How bad was it at the hostel last night?

Wyvern   It wasn't too bad. Nobody didn't get arrested.

Cutter   Did any of the police officers get injured?

Dal   No, Vince was there. It was a chit-chat show.

Merchant   That's exactly what it was.

Bell   Can't we do something in a hurry?

Merchant   It's possible if we all pull together.

Roach   So, Merchant, tell me something, aren't we all pulling together?

Wyvern   Don't ask silly questions.

Dal   That was not a silly question.

Bell   When I got up this morning, I was trying to remember one of my dreams. It was a dream that put me in the clouds to hang onto a rainbow. This day is a day of no excitement for me. I am sick and tired of the troubles and setbacks that we are having with Adventure Inside Thirteen.

Merchant   So am I, Bell.

Wyvern   That's right, man, listen.

Roach   I don't think he can.

Bell   So the fact remains, I don't even want to talk about that horrible council meeting. It was a disgrace and we all know it.

Cutter   What do you suggest we do, Bell?

Bell   I say let's put our cards on the table. Some of us is holding secrets from each other.

Dal   What do you mean?

Roach   Listen to her, Dal.

Cutter   I don't follow you, Bell. What secrets are we holding back?

Merchant   Bell can always explain herself.

Cutter   Well, let's hear some of your secrets.

Bell   Is it fair that we are lying to each other?

Wyvern   This is worse than torture. I was hoping not to talk today but Merchant should never be anywhere near Adventure Inside Thirteen.

Cutter   Come on, Wyvern. Why the hell should Mr Merchant not be on the committee?

Wyvern   Because he's a bastard, that's why.

Cutter   That's no bloody reason. I am a bastard. I have no father. He was drowned in the coalmines before he had a chance to marry my mother.

Roach   That's not what he means.

Cutter   Well, why doesn't he bloody well say what he means? Why should Mr Merchant not be involved with Adventure Inside Thirteen? Come, Wyvern, explain yourself.

Wyvern   Because he's a bastard.

Bell   Well, everyone in the whole area knows that Merchant and Wyvern and are not the best of friends.

Helen   I say for God's sake why not. They are both Black.

Cutter   I am getting nowhere with this conversation.

Roach   Helen, you must realise that not every Black and Black get on with each other.

Bell   What is the problem between Merchant and Wyvern? That was what my dream was about. I saw the both of them from my bad fighting each other in the hostel. That kind of action is a disgrace. The whole project is in jeopardy. How is the council going to give us money when you two are fighting each other publicly? Don't you know that you two are responsible citizens? What is the problem, Merchant?

Wyvern   He's a fucking bastard, that same Merchant.

Cutter   For God's sake, Wyvern, explain yourself.

Merchant   He can't. How can a moron explain himself?

Bell   Come on, Wyvern, put your cards on the table.

Dal   I think it is more than putting your cards on the table. They have a problem and we must help. I love both of them. I know they are both working for the cause. I am not suggesting that we can solve their problem with the one two strokes of the magic wand. We must help them. We are not the type of committee who would sit back and let the differences between two of our members damage the future prosperity of this project. Let's have it in the open. The majority of the committee is present.

Merchant   Our problem is a deep one.

Cutter   How deep is it? Let's talk. Put it on the table as Bell suggested.

Merchant   I would have to go back many years.

Wyvern   All I have to do is open my mouth.

Roach   At the moment Wyvern and Merchant cannot come together in this present situation.

Cutter   Bloody hell, why not? Let's have it all out, man.

Bell   As surely as the moon follows the sun and for the like of my life, I cannot work out the differences.

Helen   Well, for heaven's sake will one of you tell us something?

Wyvern   The seriousness of Merchant's sins and crimes is beyond my understanding. The man cannot see that for the love of God and all the brethrens that he himself is almost putting Black people into prison. As a matter of fact the man is a fuckin' drag. I live with the man, I know him.

Cutter   But why do you hate Mr Merchant, Wyvern?

Wyvern   Because I hate him. And if I ever like him, I would sink to the lowest level of the human race. We all agree that the Black kids need help. And I am almost wise enough to know that some of the white youths need help also.

Helen   I am surprised you said that, Bell. The National Front is no good, no bloody good at all for this country.

Bell   If they are the party that is going to help the Blacks then they can count me in.

Helen   The National Front hate the Blacks. They made that quite clear in their manifesto. There would be a local war if the National Front set foot in this playground.

Merchant   And war have never created peace. The National Front of all people. They destroy peace.

Wyvern   Shut your mouth, you have no sense. The National Front have got you working for them.

Merchant   They are only small-time. The police will soon put a stop to their racist activities.

Roach   You want to stop them yourself. Leave the police out of it. Go and fight your own battles like the youths of today.

Merchant   We at the CRC will fight the National Front in courts and around the conference table. This country is not run by racist political dictators. The Commission is expanding rapidly and more and more promotion is coming Black people's way.

Wyvern   Why do I hate you?

Merchant   I don't know. I do a bloody decent job for Black people.

Helen   The National Front is trying to bring Nazi Germany in the thirties to England in 1977.

Bell   There will never be another Hitler.

Merchant   Bell, are you supporting the National Front?

Bell   No I am not.

Merchant   Then what are you saying?

Cutter   She's only speaking her mind.

Helen   I love England and I will not allow the National Front to destroy it with their hate and destruction. My family have fought those Nazi bastards in two world wars. The imperial racist pigs are the only politicians who are capable of starting a world war. The National Front are only encouraging looting and rioting in our high streets.

Wyvern   The National Front is rich and the Blacks are poor. Maybe they need getting together. Then we would see what would happen.

Roach   The Black youths are very poor.

Helen   And so are the majority of the whites who are fighting the NF.

Roach   So it would be just another war of the poor fighting the rich for more bread.

Merchant   All my life I have been fighting for the poor man, but I cannot give my full support to this project if the committee are in sympathy with the NF.

Wyvern   If the National Front give us money for this project, I would gladly take it to help teach our youths a decent trade. Then there'll be no more fighting in the streets because all our Blacks will be working in the factories.

Helen   The NF will never allow Blacks to get a decent job in our country. If the National Front ever have any part of this project I will resign forthwith.

Wyvern   Okay, okay. What is the government policy for fighting the National Front – none.

Merchant   Shut up, boy. You want to come in our office and see the pile of information that we have on the National Front.

Wyvern   Words, words. No fuckin' action.

Helen   That is the traditional way of dealing with political thugs in this country. We will destroy the Front.

Roach   And I am sure it will be in the same manner as the Labour Party destroying the Conservative Party.

Dal   How long has this project been going on?

Bell   On and off now for five years.

Dal   You're not saying much, Cutter.

Cutter   No I am listening.

Dal   It seems to me that we have a better situation here than what we have in the States. I love my country so maybe we could succeed where my country failed. I am glad that Helen said she loved England.

Roach   Are you saying that we Blacks don't love England?

Dal   No, I am saying we are slow, slow damn slow in coming together and amongst ourselves. Let's stop fighting amongst ourselves.

Cutter   They are not fighting, they're only letting off steam. We are all together.

Dal   Well, let's talk about the project and where we are going to get the money from.

Roach   Do you have a similar project like Adventure Thirteen in the States?

Dal   Yes, but I don't know anything about it. This is the first opportunity I have had to work on a multi-racial youth scheme. Our immediate plans should be to get the kids interested enough to come back to the playground. And we must find out what the older youths think about the running of this project. There is another council meeting tomorrow. We all could go along and lobby the councillors for our grant.

Bell   I will be there.

Helen   So will I.

Merchant   Count me in.

Dal   Cutter?

Cutter   No, sorry, busy somewhere else.

Roach   Me too. I will be working with the tape recorder in the cafe.

Wyvern   I have a meeting at the hostel.

Dal   Well, that leaves Vince and Reitha. I suggest we have a proper get-together here the day after the council meeting.

Roach   What day is that?

Dal   Friday.

Cutter   This was an interesting morning. We seem to be getting somewhere. I must be off. See you all on Friday after lunch?

Dal   Yes, let's make it three o'clock, see you later.

Cutter   Yes.

Merchant   I must be getting back to the office myself. Wyvern, I would be grateful if you were not at home tonight. Perhaps we might see some sense and support my campaign against the Front. Roach, I hope you are successful with your interviews. I am all for Adventure Inside Thirteen. Bell, see you at the council meeting if not before.

Bell   Alright, Merchant. And don't overwork yourself in that office.

Merchant   Goodbye.

Helen   Wyvern, you are not a National Front man are you?

Wyvern   No I am not.

Bell   Merchant is a good worker. You must give him more respect. Okay, I know some of his ideas are old fashioned.

Helen   But nevertheless he has done a great deal for this neighbourhood. He was one of the first Blacks to stand up to fight for other Blacks.

Wyvern   The man is still fighting in the Second World War.

Bell   Yes, Merchant need more understanding. As a matter of fact he is overworked.

Dal   He's very consistent and reliable.

Wyvern   Well, I am off for a walk and then I will make it to the hostel. See you at the meeting Friday afternoon.

Roach   Right see you, Wyvern. I might catch up with you in the coffee bar later.

Wyvern   Yes, see you.

Helen   Wyvern spoke a lot today. It is a change for him. I don't believe he would support the National Front. He is just upset with Merchant.

Roach   But what is the National Front? We Blacks don't know nothing about them. They are just a bunch of white folks who go around shouting, 'No immigration. We hate the Blacks.' We are used to that kind of abuse since the first Black man set foot in this country.

Helen   They are a lot worse than that. They are evil. They are trying to destroy people like you and myself. They are bloody Big Daddy's protector.

Bell   The only trouble is, Helen, when you think about it, the Blacks in England are not very political. And over the years, we have been used as a scapegoat by every left-wing political group that ever set foot in our neighbourhood. The Blacks have got nothing to lose.

Roach   Except their headaches. Boy, I've got eyes like a hawk. The National Front might hate us, I don't know. And funny enough I have never met a white man who admits he is National Front. The left-wing groups are using us as a stepping stone to get where they are going. And God in heaven knows that I don't know where they are going. They are saying don't hurt the Blacks, they are human beings and then again all my days in England, I haven't met a single white man who admit that he hates us Blacks. As a matter of fact I haven't met a single white man who hates me because I am Black. If he hates me it is always for something else. But I know there is something else lurking underneath and it is not love or hate. Somebody somewhere in the past have planted the idea in the majority of white people's heads never to trust us Blacks. Who are the Blacks in England? Where did they come from? Some of them is from Africa, Jamaica, Guyana, Barbados, Trinidad and many more other places of the world. And then on the other hand the Indian race is a different kettle of fish. Yet the white man have successfully put all of us in the same ghetto to fight each other.

Bell Roach, you make me feel like crying. It is only the mercy of God that is stopping us from killing off each other in the ghetto.

Roach My soul have been busted wide open because of misunderstanding between brothers and brothers.

Helen I have always understood the problem of the Black from the West Indies and the majority of them come from Jamaica. I eat sleep and drink with them problem is communication. And political groups like the National Front is not making it any easier for the Blacks.

Roach And neither is the left-wing political groups.

Helen But at least we don't say we hate the Blacks. We will always want to know the problem of the Black man in the ghetto.

Roach I understand what you are saying, Helen.

Dal I have a spiritual love for each person on this project. I have learnt a lot from each individual that I have met in the neighbourhood. You are all such nice people. I am sure this project will be a success I am beginning to see some of the problems more clearly. The world is surely changing.

Roach I am going to take my tape recorder on the street. Dal, I think we will call at the hostel first and then maybe a few homes.

Dal How exciting. I've never been to the hostel. You ready?

Roach Yes.

Dal Right. Bye for now.

Roach You two take care of yourselves. See you at the meeting.

Helen Yes we will.

Bell Helen I am tired.

Helen So am I, Bell. So am I. You achieve nothing sitting on your backside. We women must do something. Men are so slow. They think of us women only in their spare time. Our emotions are different from men. We must have equal rights just like the men in this society. We are not the weaker sex as men would like us to believe. We are as strong as them if not stronger.

Reitha Hi, where is everybody?

Bell They are all gone, my dear.

Helen Where is Vince, is he at home?

Reitha No he is still in the queue at the SS. Signing on is a real drag. They are so inconsiderate in that place. I got fed up just sitting there listening to the screaming and shouting. Somebody threw a brick through the window. The police came. So I finally decided to leave. How did it go here?

Bell   We had a lovely discussion. Everybody was letting off steam, except Cutter. He only ask a few questions.

Reitha   I like him. He's tough. Vince said he's a policeman. If he is, he's a good policeman. What did you talk about?

Helen   We are going to lobby the next council meeting, tomorrow night. Can you get a few of your friends together?

Reitha   I will try.

Bell   And there will be a full committee meeting here at three o'clock next Friday.

Reitha   What is that going to be about? General chit-chat. I think we women should get more closer to each other. The men are too slow.

Helen   I agree with you.

Bell   Well, we can always try.

Reitha   Men are such a lazy bastards. Always telling us women what to do and when to do it. I must have a chat with Dal and see what we can do. This project must not fail. What a lot of violence in the area. Vince is convinced that there will be a riot if we open the playground in a hurry. I am not sure if I believe him. Is any of the kids come to the gate?

Helen   No, not since you left.

Reitha   Why don't they come back? Merchant and Wyvern can be very stubborn. We women must go to the hostel and talk to those kids ourselves. This is no ordinary adventure playground. Every one of the youths who come here is twelve years and over. Some of them are in their early twenties. Merchant and Wyvern must realise that this is a multi-racial project and not one that will solve their own political differences.

Helen   Yes, we women must get together and try to solve some of the problems away from the men.

Reitha   Let's talk about it over a drink.

Helen   That's a good idea.

Bell   I will join you myself.

Helen   Let's have a big pub lunch.

Reitha   Yes I need a drink. I need a drink.

Bell   Me too. Let's go.

Reitha   Hello. Vince, what are you doing here? There was a dozen people in front of you when I left.

Vince   The minute you walk through the door, another brick came flying through the window. And within thirty seconds a dozen pigs or more turned up. I couldn't sit in the same building with so many pigs. They look like the riot squad to me.

Bell   You mean two bricks went through the window in the same morning.

Vince   The whole building is in turmoil. I am tired but I cannot sleep. That council meeting late last night was really bad.

Bell   We are going to lobby the next one.

Vince   When is it?

Helen   Tomorrow night.

Vince   That means they are going to put up rates again. Let's give them a shock. The council is quick to collect poor people's money, yet it is taking them a lifetime to give us a few shillings for Adventure Inside Thirteen. It would be nice if some of the kids from the hostel would come along with us to the council meeting.

Helen   We were thinking we women should go to the hospital and talk to the kids ourselves.

Vince   Wyvern wouldn't like it.

Bell   We can handle him. We women are going to be much more active in this project.

Vince   I welcome the suggestion. What happened after I left?

Bell   Some of us think we should go to the NF for our money, if the council let us down.

Vince   Over my dead body. Those fascist bastards is not going to get anywhere near this project. Who suggested we go to the NF for our money, was it Cutter?

Helen   I agree with you Vince my whole body become a pillar of salt every time the NF is mentioned.

Reitha   That's interesting. I didn't know that was going on. Vince, is Cutter really a policeman?

Vince   Yes he is. I told you right after he joined the committee. I could do with a pint.

Helen   We were just about to go to the pub.

Reitha   Yes, let's go and play now tactics for tomorrow night.

Helen   Come on, come on, let's go, I will never get a bloody drink.

Vince   I am a little tired.

Helen   We know, Vince. We all appreciate your great strength. It is tough but we will make it. Relax, Vince.

Act Two

Adventure playground. Friday afternoon.

Dal What I don't understand is, why this project was named Adventure Inside Thirteen.

Roach It is a long story but I will tell you. Me and Joseph who get stabbed in the park the other day work on no less than five different projects, hoping to get a grant from the council to start an adventure playground in the neighbourhood. And failed every time. Joseph get fed up and left. Vince and Reitha comes along and decided to take over. They call the project Adventure Inside Thirteen. And we did get a grant from the council.

Dal Oh I see, that's why you call it Adventure Inside Thirteen.

Roach Yes.

Cutter Just look at the state of you lot. Here I am standing in the middle of our wars that you cause in the council office last night. Every policeman in the borough was alerted. And Vince here, he says he hates the bloody pigs. I don't like it. All the Blacks are doing is following their own tune which is none of your business.

Vince I've got a sprained ankle that put me on crutches. My work is fucked-up because of the kicking those pigs gave me in the council offices last night. The police don't have the right to beat up normal working-class people who is fighting rightfully and lawfully for their own existence. We are fighting for the rights of the working-class people of this country, the only people, as I see it, that is keeping the wheel turning.

Helen The future of this country depends on the goodwill of every citizen. We think more positively of our future councillors. We need to change them. They have the audacity to put up rates fourpence in the pound when to the best of my knowledge all they did since they went back into office is pledge their support to the GLC for increasing bus fares and tube fares. Take, take, take and give nothing back to the citizens. That is their policy. For the last six months they been promising us that they will discuss our project at the next meeting. Frankly I was pleased when Vince called them a fascist pig.

Roach So that started the trouble.

Reitha No, no, no. There was nearly a punch-up amongst themselves at the last meeting. If we didn't start shouting at them to do something about Adventure Inside Thirteen perhaps they would have had a punch-up amongst themselves. Some other councillors don't like what is happening. From now on they will take more notice of us.

Merchant But they must. I've got a broken finger. What for? This is not the first time I have experienced political violence. I will not give up this project unless I have to. I am drawn to full-time politics more and more every day.

Bell   After last night disgraceful attitude against us, I promised myself that I would never miss another council meeting until they agreed to give us some money for the project. And I intend to take my tin can with me to the next council meeting and ask them to contribute some of their expenses money towards this very good cause. I am not going to stop and start again. This is my first political punch-up and I enjoyed it.

Reitha   I feel very much at home when I come to this adventure playground. There is a good future in it for all of us, if we can stick it out. And I pray no more fights with the police inside the council house. That was the first time the police have ever throw me out of any building. I hope it is the last. I was shocked when I see the beating the police was giving to Vince and Merchant.

Roach   Well, I am going to the next council meeting with my boxing gloves on and I am going to take my tape recorder with me and let those councillors listen what the youths of 1977 have to say about them for not giving us the grant we so desperately need.

Dal   There is no doubt in my mind that we have to open up to a new frontier to this whole situation. I love this project. We must enter into new grounds . A new adventure into Adventure Inside Thirteen. Bell has made her choice of her weapon. She's got a tin can. We too must find a new weapon. There's no guarantee that the council will give us a grant. Let us therefore remove the romance that exist between the council and us. It wasn't long ago the moon was the greatest romance to us humans on this planet but it is no more a romance. The American astronauts have landed on it and returned successfully to Cape Kennedy with dust from some of the largest craters. What we must learn from the American astronauts is that we are capable of exploring our mind far beyond its normal concept. The kids in the neighbourhood need the adventure playground. We must not let them down. Money, money, money, we need money.

Vince   It is very difficult to run a project without some aid from the government. And it is even more difficult when you turn up at the council house to lobby the councillors and get beat up by the pigs before you have a chance to open your mouth. The pigs in this country is only helping this racist regime to eat more meat while the poor man can only have the dripping for his bread. I will continue fighting the council and the bloody pigs with every weapon that existed.

Merchant   Helen, how is the LIF getting on?

Helen   Fine, there is fifteen hundred pounds reserve in the kitty. I was told on the telephone this morning that we just received a nice fat cheque from a private donor.

Reitha   That's nice. So things are looking up on that side while things are going down on this side. The left and right of it all.

Roach   Maybe we should go to the city and approach some of those big businessmen. What do you think, Wyvern?

Wyvern   Man, I've got a deep headache. The hostel is on my mind. It seems to me that everybody is fooling us for their own political needs. Those kids at the hostel need me. Maybe I need them to for my own sanity. I don't seem to know what is going on here. The future of Adventure Inside Thirteen look delicate to me unless somebody pull something out of the bag.

Roach   I know what you mean. But keep heart, brother. We don't have much to lose because we don't have more than a begging bowl to help the Black youths in this country.

Bell   I am not going to give up this project. I intend to open the gates of this adventure playground for the kids again very shortly. Even if I have to run the whole project on my own.

Reitha   No, Bell, you are not alone. I am with you. Let's face it, there are no two ways about it. We must open the gates of the playground for the kids as soon as possible. I am tired of saying goodbye to everything we ever started. I'm staying right here with this project. And it is not going to be a prison or a graveyard for ever and ever.

Dal   Boy, oh boy, the council, it's slow, slow, damn slow. We are going to have an unmanageable situation. Perhaps we should use guns and go and take that over the council offices.

Merchant   I am taking a month's leave with my broken finger to go and work with LIF. We must have our own members on the council.

Wyvern   What is LIF?

Merchant   Boy, you don't know nothing. That is a political party that is going to put this country back on its feet.

Helen   LIF is London International Front. It was a political party that came together solely to fight the NF. We are not joking, we mean business. The sources we get her money from is a private one. Our books are only open to executive members. In less than two years we have had no less than three thousand members. And I am proud to say we are growing every day. There is one member of this committee who is one of our local leaders. I am glad to say, it is our own Merchant. He has worked very hard for LIF privately and sometimes publicly at the right places. Merchant and myself has travelled together as far away as Scotland to meet new members. We at LIF are very proud of the way its popularity has been growing. I am also very proud to ask any member of this committee to join us. There is no need for anyone to say yes at this minute. We are not yet public. All our efforts and achievements has been kept a close secret amongst ourselves. There are twenty-five members on the executive committee and fifty local leaders in different parts of the country. At this very minute we are conducting interviews and meetings in different regions of the country to choose another fifty local leaders. This golden opportunity is open for anyone here who is willing to join us as a local leader. Surely after last night memorable event in the council house there must be and I hope a few of you here if not all who would be willing to join us in the fight against this bureaucratic society which is condoning the National Front which is growing in popularity every day.

Cutter   It is my duty as a committee member to draw the attention of the other committee members of our original manifesto. That we would work towards full employment for all the committee members when we get our grant. We will all be needed here on this project. At the same time I can understand the frustration among some of us.

Dal We are all frustrated.

Cutter Yes I know.

Helen Cutter, it is important that we fight the National Front with all the help we can get. I am not a Christian but I pray often enough for the answers. The only way forward is to fight and keep on fighting.

Wyvern Helen, are you on the executive committee?

Helen Yes and I am also one of the founder members. Perhaps I should have explained LIF more clearly. LIF will not hinder in any way the nature of the adventure playground. We will still be working together as hard as we have done in the past. I would love to hear a yes from everyone here that he or she would join us.

Wyvern Is there a special membership for the original founders of LIF?

Helen Yes there are four of us.

Merchant Yes I am proud to say I am one of them.

Wyvern So why aren't you on one of the committee members? Anyway your business is not my business, no more forever. I am glad for the inside vision I have learned on this project. I'm also very proud to be part of Adventure Inside Thirteen. it is a good project and it needs the right people to keep it going in the right direction. It is very hard when you have to live and work in the ghetto. When you wake up in the shit and you work in shit and sooner or later everything goes wrong. And when things go wrong you need a good captain to keep the ship afloat. I admire the strength of some of the committee members. I have really learnt a lot from everyone. Adventure Inside Thirteen is a challenging project. The figure thirteen is mysterious. Sometimes it brings on a mystic smile on my face. That brings pleasure to my heart. I love to love with the whole emotion of my soul. Soul brothers. Soul sisters. There is a lot of soul in our Black youths at the hostel. I am grateful to everyone of the white committee members for working so hard to help Black people. What have revealed to me today that there will always be problem with the youth of my lifetime. Cutter, I admire your patience and your guts, but I have to break my promise.

Cutter Why what are you going to do?

Wyvern I'm going to work full time at the hostel.

Cutter Why when we need you on this project?

Wyvern I cannot serve two masters at the same time. The youth of the hostel need a trade. I am going to try and do my best for them for the rest of my life. Good luck with LIF, Helen and Merchant.

Merchant Thank you.

Cutter I understand, Wyvern.

Dal   Wyvern, it will always be a pleasure to work with you. I respect your talent. I'm sure you will be successful in your objectives.

Reitha   We are going to miss you, Wyvern.

Wyvern   Thank you, sister Reitha.

Helen   Good luck with the hostel. I hope you give LIF serious thought. We would love to have you as one of our local leaders.

Wyvern   No thanks, Helen, I'm not going to think of anything . . . everybody.

Bell   Take care, son.

Roach   I see you in the coffee bar later, man.

Wyvern   Yeah, see you.

Roach   I love Wyvern, he's a great brother.

Reitha   He's dedicated right down to his toenails.

Bell   He's got nothing else in his head except to help Black people.

Cutter   It seems to me that some more of us is getting ready to pull out of this project. This is wrong. Very wrong. Too bloody wrong for my liking. We should be thinking of opening the adventure playground now and not keeping the gates closed permanently.

Helen   Cutter you are wrong.

Cutter   No, Helen, I am not. Politics start and finish in the Houses of Parliament. We need peace. Violence is on the increase in the area. We must stop talking and take action. We must keep the youth here in the adventure playground. It is no use shouting at them through loud speakers when they are having pitch battles in the city centre.

Roach   And that is the truth. There is too much violence at public meetings.

Vince   What's the matter with you Blacks. Don't you realise you have to stop the National Front.

Cutter   Shut the yap, Vince. The playground is not a platform for drop-out politicians like yourself. I know your bloody grandfather was a coalminer.

Vince   You can't talk to me like that. I am not an ignorant pig. I know our rights. I had a proper education at university.

Cutter   Yes, you learn the ropes all right. I can see what is happening. It is getting nearer and nearer to that time when I'll be glad to see the back of you. Alright, what are you going to do about this project? It is going to be hard work for anyone who stays. But the rewards will be greater than the efforts. Okay, Wyvern has left us but the kids at the hostel will be more than glad to take advantage of the facilities that we will be able to offer them here. Let's not put the cart before the horse. Think before you jump.

Vince   I am going to jump right down the throat of some bastard.

Cutter   Helen, you must stay and see this project through, we're nearly there.

Vince   No.

Reitha   Why, Vince? What are you saying?

Vince   I am saying that it is time LIF go public. We have been in this dark far too long.

Dal   But you are not in it.

Vince   Oh yes I am. I'm one of the executive members and a very active one too.

Reitha   But you have never tell me anything about LIF.

Vince   Why should I? You are not interested in active politics.

Reitha   Well, this have put things in a different perspective.

Vince   I will stay but Helen and Merchant must go and get things moving in this neighbourhood.

Cutter   Yes, I've got it. You want to make it to the Houses of Parliament.

Vince   And why not. There is no better place to fight this fascist regime.

Reitha   You are bloody two-faced.

Dal   Things are much more difficult than I thought.

Roach   I am going for a walk I'll be back in a minute.

Bell   I will come with you.

Helen   There is no reason why this project should not go forward in the future with LIF.

Cutter   No, it bloody well will not. This adventure playground is not going to be a political battlefield for every type of dropout that comes into the area. Some of us have been working for a multi-racial harmony among the youth.

Vince   But there is no reason why they should not have their own political consciousness of their own future. People like you have to be conservative before you get your job in the first place.

Cutter   The type of dropouts like you've got no bottle. What are you, a communist or a socialist? You make me sick. What have you ever done for this country except to fill your belly from the fat of the land. The poor people of this country have been keeping punks like you. You have lived a life of luxury since you were born. If I wasn't a policeman I would kick fuck out of you. You have messed up everything for the adventure playground you and your bloody secret political group. What do you know about the Blacks.

Vince   One of the pigs that was kicking me last night was a Black bastard.

Cutter   So you're calling a coloured policeman a Black bastard and the white one pigs. They have a certain brand of margarine with the SB written on the end of the label. Boy, oh boy, that's me. Are you reading me? And I've got a small number too, MI5. We will always crack punks like you. We will also bust your arse all the way to the Old Bailey. You're a parasite to society. You live a life of luxury in university. For what? To come here and fuck up the Adventure Inside Thirteen. You bastard, you're not going to do it. We have been watching your activities very closely. You never contribute anything. You just destroy other people's minds for your own political stupidity.

Reitha   I feel sick.

Dal   What's wrong?

Reitha   Sick, sick of the impossibilities.

Dal   Come on, pull yourself together.

Reitha   Sick, sick.

Dal   Yes, right. Let's go for a walk. Come on, Reitha.

Reitha   Sick, sick.

Dal   Come on, Reitha, let's go for a walk. Don't, Reitha.

Reitha   I can't.

Dal   Yes you can.

Reitha   Bloody hell I can't.

Dal   Come on, come on, quick, Reitha.

Reitha   I can't, I bloody can't.

Dal   Oh yes, you bloody well can.

Reitha   What is happening, what's going on?

Dal   Come on, let's walk.

Reitha   Okay, okay.

Dal   We will see you in a little while. Come on, let's go.

Reitha   Okay, okay.

Dal   Sure. You must make yourself feel better.

Reitha   Yes, yes.

Dal   Right, see you in a little while.

Vince   So you find my political work stupid, do you?

Cutter   Yes, it is a bloody bad show. When you are dragging the others away from this project to satisfy your own political ends, for what? To cause more riots in the city. Yes you are stupid. Take it or leave it man. This is a bloody good project. This area of the city is suffering because of the half-hearted people like yourself and most of your language is a right bullshit. I am telling you, Vince, to stop setting up headquarters everywhere you go since you left university.

Vince   I work bloody hard.

Cutter   Yes, just cause riots in our cities. And you deliberately break up a good project like this. So you are ahead of LIF, eh?

Vince   I am only one of them.

Cutter   But you are, Vince. They haven't voted you out. Not yet. These youths are poor and don't have many places to go.

Vince   You are just another part of the machine that is talking. What's this, some sort of conscience trial?

Cutter   Vince, you believe that the entire police force of Great Britain is just one big fat pig. You call us pigs, you bastard. You see I have got to go right smack in the middle of the muck to dig out criminals like you. You think you could fool us with your ghetto language.

Helen   Are you going to charge him?

Cutter   You bastard, it really hurts me, when you try to break up Inside Thirteen. We also know you like Black women and always having them doing your subversive political works for the destruction of the country.

Vince   You are bloody mad. Subversive? I'm on crutches with a sprained ankle.

Cutter   Yes for causing a riot in the council house. It really hurts me when you try to break up Adventure Inside Thirteen.

Helen   Are you going to charge him?

Cutter   You bastard, calling us pigs. I find animals like you which is made up of one half rat, one half dog, which look under bushes and won't go out and do a proper day's work. What is going on in those universities? What do they teach you to do? To come here and up your muck on the local community. You want to bring Russia and China to England, you bastard.

Vince   I am not a bastard.

Cutter   Yes, you bloody well are. Shut up, bastard.

Vince   You're a sick pig.

Cutter   Bastard.

Vince   Yes, I'm a bastard for breaking my back for the working-class people of this country. Okay, so why am I left-wing politician?

Cutter   Shut up. You are no politician you are just a common everyday criminal. And you're getting more popular every day. We are putting a stop to people like you, Vince. Criminals must go to jail.

Vince   Criminal? Jail? I'm going to throw away this piece of stick in a minute. I have never heard so much rubbish. You guys are sick, man. I mean, I really understand.

Cutter   Bastard.

Merchant   Cutter, Cutter. This is a meeting a meeting for the future of Adventure Inside Thirteen. And so I must say my piece. I'm involved in too many projects, it is all too much for me. I may say my piece.

Cutter   We the police force of Great Britain are going to root out all your types. We shall destroy you bastards.

Vince   Stop calling me a bastard, motherfucker.

Merchant   Mr Cutter.

Cutter   Are you working for the CIA, motherfucker?

Helen   Are you going to charge him?

Cutter   Call yourself an Englishman?

Vince   You are paranoid, man. Your social conscience is blocked. Man you are just fucked-up. Man, you don't know what is going on at all. You should be dead, man, and become a permanent citizen in hell. Yes, man, you should be dead.

Cutter   Shut up. Your data in the computer reads that you were trained at university to go into local government if you were good enough. A powerful position if only you could get there. But no you want more. Like trying to be a scientist when you were only trained in the Arts Department.

Merchant   Mr Cutter, listen. Let me say something. It is very good what I'm going to say, very good indeed. My mind is made up when the going gets rough. I must move on out of this mess so that I can a proper day's work. We have come together from all different walks of life to make up this committee. It is very important to help Black youths of today. After the council house incident last night, I have been thinking, I don't want to get my fingers broken again. I want to go and help in the youngsters. We have achieved a lot for Adventure Inside Thirteen. Vince, Helen *

Vince   Jesus Christ, why?

Helen   Come on, Merchant, we've been working together for a long time. You can't just pull out like that. What about us? We have built and made LIF into a respectable political organisation. Not an organisation of criminals as Cutter would have us believe. It would be a bloody shame if you leave us.

Merchant   Helen, I am not leaving, I am your friend.

Helen   And so am I. You want to tell me that you're willing to just throw up everything. And all the hard work you have put into LIF. We pledge our support for

---

* Due to the age and scarcity of the original manuscripts, this section of the playtext has unfortunately been lost to time.

all the Blacks. We want to help your people to help themselves. And not to have people like Cutter breathing down their necks. The police brutality at the council house was a disgrace to any decent citizen. And you are giving up LIF? I don't believe it. Why merchant? So you can work full time for Adventure Inside Thirteen.

Merchant   No, Helen, I am giving up urban politics.

Vince   So that's the way you operate.

Merchant   I am going back to my place at the CRC. After all that is what the government paid me for.

Helen   You are talking shit.

Merchant   Okay, okay, I know what I mean. Goodbye, everybody.

Helen   You mean you just walk out on us like that.

Vince   Yes, yes, he's gone.

Cutter   And he will never return to your arms.

Helen   We at LIF have never undermined this project. The running of this project. Vince has worked bloody hard since he has been with us and recently he has worked for nothing.

Cutter   Nothing? He's getting twenty-three pounds a week from the Health Department. That is a salary of nearly twelve hundred a year tax free.

Helen   That is not the right way to look at the situation. * Front to take over the country. Vince worked a damn sight harder than half our big fat bosses.

Cutter   Vince and his likes are parasites. They are always disrupting what other people have started.

Helen   Come, come, Cutter, you don't mean that.

Cutter   Yes I do. Calling our coloured policeman Black bastards and calling us pigs.

Helen   Surely that is not what is bothering you.

Cutter   The area need the adventure playground now. The gates have been closed for far too long and there is trouble at the hospital ever since. And on top of it, he cause a bloody riot in the city last night.

Helen   Are you saying that our Vince is the cause of all the trouble in the neighbourhood?

Cutter   Yes and he will continue to do so if we don't stop him.

Helen   Cutter, this is 1977. It is not the sixteenth-century imperialist heaven. You're talking to Vince as if you have broken the Official Secrets Act.

---

* Due to the age and scarcity of the original manuscripts, this section of the playtext has unfortunately been lost to time.

Cutter   Yes he has. He was sabotaging this project while he was living pretty comfortably from the proceeds of his government salary and a big fat one he gets too for ten months.

Helen   This is a political battle not a criminal offence.

Cutter   He wants to start a riot the most all the Blacks in the city.

Vince   I am leaving Adventure Inside Thirteen. Bloody hell.

Cutter   I told you that I would be glad to see the back of you.

Vince   I would rather go and live in General Amin's country than work on the same committee as yourself. You are just a fascist imperialistic pig.

Cutter   I am going to put you in exile and give you nothing for your problems.

Reitha   * since I left university is to start rioting amongst the Blacks. I am leaving Thirteen.

Reitha   I expect you would do that.

Vince   I would never work with him.

Dal   Yes the room was pretty hot when we left.

Reitha   What are you going to do?

Vince   I am going to stir up so much shit, I am going to take this country and shake it by its throat. LIF is going to cause so much trouble the imperialist pigs would be begging us to have mercy on them. LIF is going to places and a month after we go public, it will become one of the major political parties in the country. Jail me if you like I don't care. My grandfather was more than a coalminer. He went to prison for his rights. We at LIF will not stop until we smash every imperialist bastard in this country.

Reitha   I am sorry you are leaving, Vince.

Vince   I am not. I am glad to see the back of the likes of him.

Dal   Now that Vince is going, who is going to be in charge?

Reitha   The arse of Adventure Inside Thirteen have been busted wide open. The youths in this area will have another long wait for the adventure playground.

Helen   I have a feeling perhaps, we are all working for the same cause in different ways. There is two sides to a coin.

Bell   I am tired of protesting with banners in the city centre and picketing town halls. I am going to do something I've always wanted to do. I have made a good choice and I am sure I will have the support of the committee. I am moving on and live on a different level with the world. I am going to change my relationship with the area and

---

* Due to the age and scarcity of the original manuscripts, this section of the playtext has unfortunately been lost to time.

start my own monthly newspaper. There is a need for a much wider* Things get too crowded sometimes. Some of us need to break away. I want to do something for my people before it is too late and above all I want to spend more time with my grandchild.

Helen   I'm glad you finally take the plunge, Bell.

Dal   Bravo, we could do with another newspaper.

Reitha   You have made a good choice, Bell.

Bell   Thanks.

Reitha   If you ever need a helping hand, I'm always available.

Cutter   We will all chip in if you need us.

Bell   Good luck with LIF, Helen.

Helen   And the same to you, Bell. I will pay you a visit before your first issue.

Bell   Thank you all. And now I am going home for a rest. Bye.

Reitha   So, Vince, you are leaving.

Vince   I was forced to take such drastic action.

Helen   More like he's been kicked out to me.

Cutter   All your politics is, Vince, is to call yourself a socialist, so you can fool the poor citizens in making promises to them that you can put a few more pounds and their pay packets. And at the same time putting their souls into your own prison. We are the people who put people into prison, not you. All you do is cause trouble.

Helen   Vince is a political genius. He's a man of the seventies and eighties.

Roach   Well, well, well. So the project gets stuck again. I have never had time for big politics in this country. I am leaving Adventure Inside Thirteen. But I'm not leaving the playground. Not yet. Not until the gates are open to the public again. I've got a tape recorder, so I'm going to broaden my outlook on life. Bell is starting up a newspaper. I am going to finish the slope and become the odd job man on a part-time basis. The youth in the area need the playground. I've got nothing more to say. I am off to work on the slope.

Vince   So you are going to put me in exile.

Helen   Vince is one of the new breed of politicians that this country badly needs.

Cutter   And I see it that the country is breeding a new kind of criminal that will run the country into a standstill before the eighties.

Reitha   I want to sing the blues because I just don't know what to do with myself. Oh my God, daddy's gone fishing for food, mammy's out shopping for door handles,

---

* Due to the age and scarcity of the original manuscripts, this section of the playtext has unfortunately been lost to time.

the house is empty, brother is working on the railroad, sister is down the road selling buttons and my man is in jail. I just don't know what to do.

Dal   It has been a hard day on all of us. We need space and time to think about the future. Let's just cool it before we become enemies of each other.

Vince   Cutter, you remind me of those gigantic men that they feature in comic strip. One minute he removes the mountain with his hands and the next is reduced to fuck-all.

Cutter   Are you threatening me?

Helen   No he's not. He's merely letting off steam.

Cutter   Snap out of it, Helen. Always think before you jump. We need you here at the playground.

Helen   No, Cutter, I have already taken the jump.

Cutter   Helen, I don't think you understand. You are only infatuated with Vince.

Helen   Come, come now, Cutter. I've been in politics all my life and I'm pretty satisfied with LIF. My mind is made up, I'm in the running for the full-time. I see no better way to fight the front.

Vince   Bloody hell, we will smash those imperialist pigs.

Reitha   Are you leaving us for the good, Helen?

Helen   I thought I made myself quite clear when I asked the rest of you to join me at LIF.

Dal   You have been a great inspiration to all of us so you were not going to do it all the way in one minute.

Cutter   Helen, I don't want to be heavy handed with you. The police in this country have never stood in the way of any political group. But when you have actors like Vince who have done nothing since he left university except increase the Blacks in the vicinity to rise against the police.

Vince   I'm going to smash your face in a minute with these crutches.

Cutter   Go on hit me, you bastard, hit me. Call yourself an Englishman. Hit me.

Vince   I will kill you.

Reitha   Stop it, Vince.

Vince   Shut up. Don't you see what this bastard is doing to me?

Reitha   I can't help you.

Vince   Oh so you're on his side are you?

Reitha   No I am not on any bloody sides. I'm trying to stop you from getting yourself into more trouble.

Vince   What trouble?

Reitha   I am for the playground.

Vince   I have worked bloody hard for your people in opening their eyes to the danger of this fascist bastards in this country.

Cutter   Yes like going to the hostel and opening their eyes to riot amongst themselves and the police.

Vince   I am going to kill you.

Cutter   Go on, you bastard, hit me. Hit me, you subversive coward.

Vince   Okay, Cutter, I am going but the fight has only just begun. You haven't heard the last of this.

Cutter   For the last three years, we know every time you have a crap.

Vince   Yes that is all you are capable of. Spying on other people's private lives. I'm going to continue to work for what I believe in. I'm going to LIF to work full-time. You are not going to have everything your own way. I'm leaving for good. Are you coming, Reitha?

Reitha   I'm not going any further into politics.

Vince   You are going to stay here and work with him? It is people like him who are sitting on top of your brothers and sisters and keeping them in basement flats up and down the country. How can you work for a person who is working for the secret service.

Reitha   I'm not working for anybody. I am working for the playground.

Vince   If you continue to work for Adventure Inside Thirteen you will be working for the secret service.

Reitha   I am not leaving this project come hell or heaven put together. I am not leaving this very playground. I cannot work with you or LIF which I know nothing about until today. While the gates of this playground remain closed to the public, I will not leave it until it is open.

Vince   We at LIF are fighting people like Cutter for the Blacks.

Reitha   I always wondered if you love me or not.

Vince   So what's this then, are we splitting up?

Reitha   I don't know. It's up to you.

Dal   This is not the right place to talk about things like that.

Vince   Yes it is bloody well okay by me, if that's the way you want it. Right, I am going. Reitha, you know where to find me if you want me.

Reitha   What do you mean?

Vince   I will be at LIF, Reitha.

Reitha   Where is LIF?

Cutter   You mean the basement at 64? That place don't exist, Vince. We were there last night when you were at the council house. All the files with the public prosecutor. There's a twenty-four-hour guard outside the door. Take my advice, don't go anywhere near the place.

Vince   Fuck your advice.

Helen   Why, Cutter, what's the charge?

Cutter   I don't know, Helen. I'm only doing my job.

Helen   But you can't do that to the LIF. And leave people like the National Front to run around waving the Union Jack.

Cutter   It is out of my hands, Helen. It is up to the public prosecutor what charges should be pressed against Vince.

Helen   But you must charge me too.

Cutter   No one has been charged.

Helen   I demand to see your superior.

Cutter   It's up to you, Helen. They are down Whitehall.

Helen   Whitehall?

Cutter   Yes. That's how much trouble these modern subversive politicians of the seventies like Vincent G. A. Longburn are causing the Foreign Office.

Vince   I am going to murder you.

Cutter   Go on hit me, hit me. You rat, call yourself an Englishman.

Vince   You bloody git.

Helen   Cutter, over the course of one morning, you have moved up from being an ordinary policeman, all the way up to the Foreign Office.

* three years that Vince is working for the KGB.

Reitha   No, no, he is not working for the KGB.

Cutter   Reitha, you didn't even know he was head of LIF.

Helen   I don't believe none of this rubbish.

Dal   No I don't believe Vince is working for the KGB.

Cutter   I hope he's not for his sake.

Vince   I can't take any more of this rubbish I'm going.

Cutter   Where are you going?

---

* Due to the age and scarcity of the original manuscripts, this section of the playtext has unfortunately been lost to time.

Vince   None of your bloody business. Can't you see if I don't go I'm going to murder you.

Cutter   I told you, I would be glad to see the back of you.

Vince   Yes and not a minute too soon, you haven't seen the last of me.

Cutter   Yes I know.

Vince   Don't give in to him, Helen.

Helen   I won't.

Vince   See you later, Reitha.

Reitha   Yes.

Cutter *into walkie-talkie.*

Cutter   'West End central over.'

Radio   Receiving you ten twenty-two over.

Cutter   'Vincent George Alexander Longburn have just left the playground on crutches over.'

Radio   We have made contact over.

Cutter   'Over and out.'

Helen   You have broken a good soldier.

Cutter   Yes I know but all soldiers should be in the army.

Helen   Well, if Vince is in trouble, it is my duty to stand by him.

Cutter   Helen, you're welcome to stay and continue to help run the playground.

Helen   No, the playground is not for me. You cannot fight the NF sitting on your backside.

Cutter   Helen? We have smashed LIF. We also know that you were not involved in all its activities like some of the other members.

Helen   Then I must start again. I will never give up active politics.

Cutter   Nobody asking you to give up at the politics. You must admit yourself that some of the LIF tactics are pretty pathetic. Some of your members are potential dropout.

Helen   Never.

Cutter   Violence leads to murder.

Helen   You should blame the National Front for the violence.

Cutter   Helen, we have got information on quite a number of different political groups up and down the country. Some of them are many times larger than LIF. If we don't put a stop to some of their activities, there will be looting and burning on some of our major high streets. This whole business is coming from cabinet level. We just don't have the men to cope with large-scale riots like they have in the United States.

Dal   Yes, we do have some large ones at home.

Helen   Cutter, we are on different sides of the fence. I have enjoyed working with you. You are a courageous young man and no doubt you will go far. I haven't enjoyed what you have done to Vince and as you put it smash LIF. I am a woman and I love my country as much as any blueblood Englishman. I shall continue to work for LIF all the way to my rocking chair. Dal, will you join me reshaping LIF.

Dal   Thanks, Helen. But no I love working with kids.

Helen   there is nothing left for me to * people like me don't have to be bad or good.

Helen   Thank you, Dal.

Dal   Helen, I'm sorry to see you leave.

Helen   Come on, come on, why all this sadness?

Dal   You are such a lovely person.

Helen   Oh be off with you. You take care of yourselves. We are proud to have you in our neighbourhood. Reitha, now you must always keep trying, always fight for your rights.

Reitha   Helen, every Black person that I know in the neighbourhood respect you. You have done a lot for us, my God I love you for it.

Helen   Your people are one of the nicest things that ever happened to me.

Dal   We all love you, Helen.

Helen   Thank you. Goodbye.

Cutter   Dal, will you go and get Roach.

Reitha   What about Vince? What's going to happen to him?

Cutter   I am sorry I can't discuss Vince with you.

Reitha   God it's really painful.

Cutter   Yes I know. I am sorry.

Reitha   Is he in trouble?

Cutter   He hasn't been charged.

Reitha   No, no. Yes, yes. When and where did it start? You don't believe he's working for the KGB do you?

Cutter   No I don't believe he's working for the KGB.

Reitha   Well, thank God for that.

Cutter   Vince is what he is. I can't change the situation. Sometimes I don't like my job.

---

* Due to the age and scarcity of the original manuscripts, this section of the playtext has unfortunately been lost to time.

Reitha   So why do you do it?

Cutter   I love my country.

Reitha   That's good. Everybody should love their country.

Roach   Yes, Cutter.

Cutter   How's the slope coming along?

Roach   Alright. I should finish it by tomorrow.

Cutter   Well, there's only four of us left.

Dal   I feel awful but I am not going to run away.

Cutter   I didn't think you would.

Roach   I understand that perhaps Vince is in serious trouble.

Cutter   We don't know.

Reitha   I thought I knew everything about Vince.

Dal   Well, you didn't and that's that. Women have to learn to pick themselves up from under the feet of men and stand on their own two feet.

Cutter   I'm sorry I kept my identity a secret from some of the committee members. Vince knew that I was a policeman before I join the committee.

Reitha   What?

Cutter   Oh yes. But you didn't know what kind of policeman I was. Mind you, I don't see why you shouldn't have a local bobby on your committee.

Roach   Why did you join us?

Cutter   Because Vince convinced the rest of you that the National Front was coming to smash up the playground. And then have a cheek to close the gates. And he nearly succeeded since he started his latest activities. We have nothing but trouble in the area since he closed the gates for his own political reasons. That makes him a rat as far as I'm concerned. Reitha, how much money is it in the kitty?

Reitha   Well, let's see. The last bank statement we had we were overdrawn two thousand pounds.

Cutter   What's the limit?

Reitha   Three thousand five hundred. I would say offhand that we have approximately four to five hundred.

Cutter   Not bad. Things could be a lot worse we are not in the * night's disturbance didn't help. I was told offhand recently and what I am going to say is not official that Adventure Inside Thirteen will be getting twenty to twenty-five thousand from urban aid.

---

* Due to the age and scarcity of the original manuscripts, this section of the playtext has unfortunately been lost to time.

Dal   That's fantastic.

Cutter   Roach, what's your opinion of a local bobby joining the committee.

Roach   It's got nothing to do with me, I resigned from the committee.

Cutter   Oh yes, I almost forgot. Me too, Roach. So, Reitha, it's up to you and Dal. My advice to both of you is that you continue to pay Roach his normal wages and you and Dal make do with the rest until you get your grant. Don't worry you'll get it. I must move on. So, Roach, if I work with you on the slope we could finish it today.

Roach   Yes.

Cutter   Here are the keys, Reitha. Right, Roach, let's go.

Reitha   Let's go and open the gates.

Dal   Yes.

Wings singing 'Let 'Em In'.

Blackout.

Four Hundred Pounds

Characters

Bees, *age thirty-two, Jamaican*
Tecee, *age thirty-six, Jamaican*

Play set in Finsbury Park, London.

Bees' room recently painted. One stool, one bench, one chair, pool table. One table in corner with electric kettle, half bottle of whisky, brandy, rum, one case of Red Stripe beer, Special Brew. A few empty cans scattered around the floor. Mop bucket and broom. Dart board on wall with six darts stuck in it. **Tecee** *runs into room with* **Bees** *close behind. They are wearing identical clothes – roll-neck pullover with waistcoat, smart pair of trousers, skullcap.* **Tecee** *with donkey-jacket in his hand,* **Bees** *is wearing his.* **Tecee** *sits on bench, his knees bent, clutching his coat,* **Bees** *walking the room.*

Bees   Tecee, why didn't you sink the black? I don't believe it, you sink the white instead. I witness a deliberate crime against me.

Tecee   Four hundred years all end in one day.

Bees   It was four hundred pounds.

Tecee   The white, the red, the black plus the other colours – it's too much.

Bee   That's what our life is about.

Tecee   I know – that's why I want to know why we have to use the white to sink the black.

Bees   We can't use the red.

Tecee   A change, which way does the world spin?

Bees   From East to West.

Tecee   That is neither left nor right.

Bees   Why do you want to know?

Tecee   I want to meet all the people.

Bees   Where, in your head?

Tecee   Yes, I want to ask them a question.

Bees   What question?

Tecee   A favourable question in my interests.

Bees   When are you going to start?

Tecee   Any day now.

Bees   You'd better make an early start or you will mad me with your stupidity.

Tecee   I feel a very powerful calling to do something else. I did what I did for some force much bigger than myself. I feel sick about my innocent deed but my heart is relieved.

Bees   Do I know you?

Tecee   Yes.

Bees   That's not a very good lie – try again.

Tecee   You don't know me.

Bees   Not bad, but your mind have got to be investigated. (*He takes off his coat and hangs it up.*) I just have to know which way your mind is going.

Tecee   Who is going to do the investigation?

Bees   Me of course.

Tecee   I hear you knocking.

Bees   That's not true, I am in.

Tecee   I have to get a good job.

Bees   You're good at fucking up my head.

Tecee   What should I do about it.

Bees   You should have sink the black.

Tecee   Too late, brother – the white takes the money and gone.

Bees   Let me think. (*His face in his hands.*) Yes, I met someone like you once before I met you.

Tecee   Are you sure?

Bees   Yes.

Tecee   I don't know what to think about that.

Bees   It doesn't matter what you think, I know what I think.

Tece   Bees, I want to do something else.

Bees   The money.

Tecee   Man, the world a change.

Bees   Are you changing?

Tecee   What do you think?

Bees   I don't know.

Tecee   Yet you know so much about me not sinking the black.

Bees   Man, stop the foolishness.

Tecee   As far as I can see we only ever talk about money.

Bees   Isn't that the reason we work together?

Tecee   This is not my day.

Bees   That's right, you don't own the day.

Tecee   People like you think they own the day and other people's freedom.

Bees   Don't fuck with me, man.

Tecee   Yeah, yeah.

Bees   I am discovering something about you.

Tecee   Something new?

Bees   It is as old as the hills.

Tecee   How old are the hills?

Bees   Very old.

Tecee   Alright, old-timer.

Bees   You could have sink the black. Nothing wrong with your co-ordination. I don't know what to say, you take my life out of my body and give it away.

Tecee   You can't resist talking fuckries, can you?

Bees   I am going to be your witness for the next D-Day.

Tecee   Are you going to be the executioner as well?

Bees   You are very wicked, you same Tecee.

Tecee   What else you do these days other than talk to me?

Bees   Nothing, I am a gambler – my interest is in the pool table.

Tecee   There is no future in that business for us.

Bees   Oh yes there is.

Tecee   How, this room doesn't even belong to us – it's the squatters them control the building.

Bees   That's alright, I'm only interested in the pool table.

Tecee   Life is really funny. I am tired of living on a limb so I want to have more sense.

Bees   What about your Bible? You don't get enough sense from that?

Tecee   I done with this life – I finish with nervousness. I wonder how Jamaica is?

Bees   Why, you thinking of going down there today?

Tecee   Yes, I homesick.

Bees   I just don't know where to start – all I know is that we have to talk or fight. I just don't know which road to take on this very day with you.

Tecee   You could get gambling out of your head for a start.

Bees   Shut up – why didn't you sink the black?

Tecee   I have changed, you know how I have been feeling.

Bees   No, I don't, you idiot.

Tecee   I just don't know what to think. When people call me idiot for telling them the truth so I feel seh after this episode something nice is going to happen to me.

Bees   It already has.

Tecee   So how comes I don't know nothing about it?

Bees   Yes you do – it's me.

Tecee   How will I ever pay you?

Bees   You don't have to – just show your appreciation that I haven't kill you.

Tecee   Black people life in England always seems to end up this way in places like this. I done with the fucking gambling places them.

Bees   Perhaps is the English ghost and the Jamaican Dobya dem dat are fucking your head.

Tecee   Is that what you think I am?

Bees   Yes. This place is haunted you know that.

Tecee   I have heard talking.

Bees   So you hear the ghosts them a talk? Ah, that's what happened to your head.

Tecee   What a way your face light up about ghosts – I feel say you want to be a hobya man with my blood.

Bees   No, I feel like a spaceman is have to put up with you on Earth.

Tecee   Some more of them is going to land one day to collect you.

Bees   I know and I'm making good preparations for them. This part of the universe is certainly not my home after what you did to me today.

Tecee   Maybe your love for a better life in this part of the universe is not as strong as mine so I want to tell you: the first thing is my mind is following my feelings – that's why I couldn't sink of the black.

Bees   Are you saying the black ball represents Black people in your head – look at me, Tecee – I am not even angry, not shouting or laughing. I want to listen to you – tell me more.

Tecee   I man is thinking that I must get up and do something good for mankind.

Bees   That's a very difficult thing to do for a person who talk about Jesus and gamble at the same time. The black was a sitting duck – all that money.

Tecee   It seems to me that a person can do very little for their friend unless they can afford to give them some money, so perhaps if I did rob a bank and give you the money you would have understand what I've been trying to tell you for months.

Bees   I wonder if there's any available force in the universe to tell me what happened in that pool room today.

Tecee   Yes, turn to Jesus.

Bees   Jesus doesn't mean anything to me other than somebody write about Him in a book.

Tecee   That's a sin.

Bees   Just listen to me while I try to tell you something – when was I ever interested in Jesus? When I want answers for a question that I can't answer in my head I go and work it out on the computer. Logic say the computer is good for mankind.

Tecee   So was Jesus.

Bees   They killed him, nobody can kill the computer.

Tecee   Yes, true, Jesus did have a heart and He bleed blood on the cross and so far nobody have pumped blood into the computer.

Bees   There is some sense in that but it's not logic. My head, the money.

Tecee   Is logic a Christian?

Bees   No it's a word with a lot of sense.

Tecee   Well, the only understanding I ever come to with you is that you are waiting for unidentified flying spaceman and I am waiting for Jesus. Perhaps Jesus and the spaceman will arrive at the same time – boy, a disc jockey have a good job. They work people's emotions and machine together.

Bees   I have no choice but to find out what's wrong with your head. Do you know who owns this building?

Tecee   No.

Bees   It's the government.

Tecee   I am not surprised, they own a lot of buildings.

Bees   You know they're watching us.

Tecee   If the building belongs to them – yes.

Bees   Man I think you a dream in your wickedness.

Tecee   That's possible, but I am not asleep.

Bees   You are saying nothing except rubbish – and all that money is lost on one game of pool – I bet I take up something and lick you down – I tired of asking you why you never sink the black ball, is some sense I trying to get out of you – that's why I am still talking to you, you useless bloodclaat – I fucking hate you. This is your last chance with me.

Tecee   And I is trying to tell you that I win my last chance. I stop gamble, done with it. Gambling is driving us mad, let's use the government building for something else other than selling booze and playing pool – I tell you it was Jesus's hand that reach across the table and stop me from sinking the black ball. The Lord is moving sideways in my heart and anywhere He is Jesus is standing up straight.

Bees   Your mouth is fucking up your head, for to believe the way you think I might as well start talking to the spacemen before they land. I am trying to find out if you are a traitor or not. You throw away the game with the four hundred pounds and the rest.

Tecee   I told you to stop the big betting, the system have all of us immigrants gambling day and night.

Bees   Stop the fuckry! Some Black people are born in a job and they're going to die in a job.

Tecee   There is no Black man like that in England. All the Blacks in England suffer under the hands of the white man.

Bees   That's a bloody stupid excuse – when you lay down arms and let to white man trample all over you in a game of pool.

Tecee   I stop gamble that's no excuse.

Bees   You could have win the game and stop with the money four hundred pounds plus the rest – I stick to raas!

Tecee   Yes, man, four hundred this week – how much would it be next week? You must start think of doing something else – what about our children?

Bees   We haven't got any money to do anything for our children. Something is wrong with your head and it's got nothing to do with Jesus, get in the witness box.

Tecee   I am in the witness box. (*He's getting slightly hysterical.*)

Bees *at last thinks he has made a breakthrough and with great excitement he climbs and stands on the stool with hands in trouser pockets.*

Tecee   Go on, question me till kingdom come and if you have eyes you will see what I am saying, I trying to tell you that I stop gamble, I been trying to tell you for a long time and all the time you believe you would clean up every pool room in the whole wide world. I keep telling you to let us get a job before half the country's unemployed.

Bees   You're a idiot. There have never been any jobs for us since we got the sack, anyway I've got a few more questions to ask you.

Tecee   Ask me any question. I feeling free to do what I want to do for my future.

Bees   Why did you not sink the black hole?

Tecee   Jesus stopped me.

Bees   Did He talk to you before the game?

Tecee   He talks to me all the time.

Bees   How often?

Tecee   I don't know.

Bees   Did He talk to you today?

Tecee   What do you mean?

Bees   Well, let me put it this way, did He take you to one side while I wasn't looking and say, 'Hey, Tecee, the four hundred pounds that belongs to you and Bees, you must lose it on this very game of pool'?

Tecee   Bees, what are you trying to do? Did I tell you to bet so much money?

Bees   No, but we are partners and I been waiting to play a game like that for a long time. When was the last time Jesus talked to you?

Tecee   Just now.

Bees   I am not Jesus.

Tecee   If you want to gamble pool find someone else as your partner and you can have this place all by yourself. I getting serious with my life – what else you want to ask me?

Bees   Why do you let a Black man down? – who have always been kind and nice to you. I am your friend and you become the biggest enemy in my life. (**Bees** *gets angry as if he is going to hit* **Tecee**. *He grabs a brandy bottle instead and smashes it on the floor.*) You like brandy so drink it off the floor. I want to cut your throat with the pieces – I have never feel like this before you are bringing hell down on me. I am going to take out the biggest insurance policy for my woman and picany. You are bringing down hell on me. (*He grabs a can of beer and throws it at* **Tecee**.)

Tecee   (*runs across room toward* **Bees** *shouting and screaming*)   You want to kill me, eh! Take every raascaat out of me, yes take my life. Take it. (**Tecee** *shows his chest in defiance.*)

Bees   Fuck off – why did you lose the game of pool?

Tecee   It's you cause me to do it – you want me to be a gambler all my life – we must find something better to do for the children's sake.

Bees   I don't find any fault with money.

Tecee   As Black people we have to start looking at what else is going on around us other than having a few pounds and in our pockets – our spirit needs food too.

Bees   There is no future in England for any spirit with no money – is money that put man in space and some of them walk on the moon. Are you listening to me? We don't move one bomboclath inch until we straighten it out – if you are mad, I am not.

Tecee   I can't feel sorry for you because you don't have no soul.

Bees   You feel sorry for me?! Don't make me laugh, you think other people is full moon, well, I am no moon. I is just a wise Jamaican and they is longer than rope. I finally catch up with you today, you see how your eye them a turn red. All that money, I feel like me head a jump off me body.

Tecee   Is you same one tell me that my eyes them a turn red and I don't know what colour they was before – all I know is that they change.

Bees   Wake up and talk sense!

Tecee   Man, shut up.

Bees   Is who you talking to?

Tecee   I don't know any more.

Bees   It's me – Bees – to raas.

Tecee   Yes, I stop gamble.

Bees   I mean to do business with you today, big colossal business. You turn and run like a chicken when the pressure hold you, you mash up me life, man. I mad to raas. What a monkey raasclaat idiot.

Tecee   I telling you to leave the pool room them alone and go and look work before it's too late.

Bees   Unemployment is the workforce of the country.

Tecee   Then Jesus is my saviour. I sinking no black ball that looks like Black people.

Bees   You mean you really believe that.

Tecee   Yes.

Bees   You're a Black man, you can't be that stupid.

Tecee   I man is only saving my soul. Man we want a better love than these kind of love.

Bees   You know that there is a microphone and midget little computer a listen to every word you are saying. I see a lot of Black men turn fool before but you beat all of them. Look how many hours we've spent together practising the shot to sink the black. I watch you shoot from morning to night and you have never missed such an easy shot as that before. You've a lot of excuse to make before the squatters get here this evening. A gambler call four hundred pounds, which slave ever own four hundred pounds. I feel seh you're onto something big and you won't tell me what it is.

Tecee   I feel seh you can't see at all when a man change. You put all that money on the game of pool, all of me see is white people, red people, Black people 'pon the pool table.

Bees   A lie you a tell, nothing na go so – you got something else on your mind, man – you're mad, but you're not that mad because me's twice as mad as you when it comes to serious business. I want to understand what's wrong with you that I never seen before.

Tecee   Change your ways and you will see how right I am.

Bees   For what?

Tecee   To do better things with my life other than play pool in this place.

Bees   Come down to earth, man, we're not in space yet.

Tecee   I down, that's why I want to get four hundred out of my head and I seh nothing would happen until I do something drastic when all eyes was looking at me. And it comes a time when I find I want more strength to learn about the people of this country.

Bees   So you don't think that I is a serious Black man? Those two idiots should never beat us at pool – I want to play the same game over with you and I want you to show me which part of the table the Black red white people dem day stand up. I never see them?

Tecee   Yes, I will.

Bees   Yes you will what?

Tecee   Play the same game with you.

Bees   I would sink that shot with my eyes closed.

Tecee   Well, close them then and let's play the game.

Bees   Set them up.

Tecee   I can't, is you got the key.

Bees   So you can't afford fifteen pence for your own pool table.

Tecee   No.

Bees   How long have we been friends?

Tecee   Many years.

Bees   Too many to count I suppose.

Tecee   Look, something that happened to me and I hope we will both benefit from it.

Bees   To separate our future at this stage in life when things is picking up for us again seems very stupid to me.

Tecee   At this moment in time what is stupid for you is wise for me.

Bees   So I have made a mistake and make myself available as your friend.

Tecee   Regrets will make you a bigger fool than what you are.

Bees   I have just pinch myself so I know I am alive, I can't give what I haven't got – so what next?

Tecee   You know if I was a good swimmer I don't know what I would do – I mean now, right now – water, water, swim, swim – I don't feel the blues I just looking and feeling the atmosphere. I answer the question right as the teacher did ask me once – I sure the wheel of fortune is still spinning and my heart used to beat faster than how it is beating now. To feel sick when I am healthy could only be pressure from you; we work seven years for the same white man, repairing cars in London – and five out of that was in night school, me studying how to be a better mechanic and you looking at computers, working out wind speed and how to get a car round again faster than any other racing driver. What a team we was then.

Bees   And then what happened? The boss man catch us playing dominoes when we should be repairing old cars and sack us on the spot.

Tecee   And take the same pack of dominoes that cause us to get the sack and went gambling on the streets – from provisional racing team to professional gambling team.

Bees   Yes, I am a proud gambler – it's better than breaking into banks and going to jail.

Tecee   Man I work hard enough to give myself a choice in life.

Bees   What choice? To give away a whole heap of money to two amateur pool players?

Tecee   And I am giving up this place as well, although I use a sledgehammer with the squatters to break the door down.

Bees   Yes, and they will legally get it off the government for themselves alone if you keep dropping me in the shit.

Tecee   Bees, I know what I want to do with my life and this place and pool doesn't come into it anymore.

Bees   We've been working with the squatters for two years keeping this building going.

Tecee   Well, let them keep it, some of them live here and we will live in our own house.

Bees   When I stop racing cars and you stop being a mechanic, that was the end of the conventional life for us; that's why we join up with the squatters them. From school days we was a team – you the mechanic, I the driver. Remember the first car we shared together in Jamaica?

Tecee   How could I forget?

Bees   But you have.

Tecee   Now all I know is that we made a bad mistake when we grab everything from Jamaica to come here to become world-class racing drivers – and anyway, I glad the white man sack us – I don't think you would be a successful racing driver.

Bees   Fuck off, I would and I would retire rich by now.

Tecee   Bees, stop dreaming. You are only going from one hill to the next.

Bees   Yes, and the next hill I come to I am going to open the biggest club on top of it.

Tecee   Yes, one day it all come to the end like a blast of thunder.

Bees   So what about your garage that you start building at the back?

Tecee   The past is dead for a few more decades.

Bees   Is not the past that's dead, is you that's dead.

Tecee   Boy, you must read God's good Bible.

Bees   Why should I? There is no way I could justify my life as being perfect. We went into this business with our eyes open and now it is downhill for our relationship, but relationship is important no more and them wham. One black ball finish the lot. And to think we both decide to leave the white man's education and slave labour alone. Like you said, we came into this business with our eyes wide open after we worked seven years for the same white man repairing old cars.

Tecee   All raasclaat right, also the Bible pool – so pool is a good games, yes, and I like it too. The adrenaline run many a time when I feeling good and so I play a good game of pool, sometime inside a lot of hate and love and hate. And love and hate is patrolling the streets day and night. Looking at the way we was when we was young and drive a car on narrow roads in Jamaica. Is Bees them did call you then and is Bees I still call you, so sometime the road get wide and then suddenly it narrows again. Is life, himself a try to find peace as far as I can see.

Bees   Which is not very far.

Tecee   Right now four hundred pounds and four hundred years is the same to me.

Bees   That was when I was dead before I was born.

Tecee   I might as well admit to a fact, I don't know what you're talking about.

Bees   Since when?

Tecee   What?

Bees   Since when you don't understand me?

Tecee   Jesus Christ! Is that a question?

Bees   Just look at the past, everybody let us down, white and Black alike. The Bible is one of the books that they used to enslave our mind and heart when we were children. (*He grabs* **Tecee** *by the shoulder.*) Talk to me, good brother, why do you want to carry other people burden?

Tecee   I not carrying no man's burden. Take your hands off me!

Bees   Maybe you think seh you did a carry me, that's why you give away the game of pool.

Tecee   Now, I want to stop before it's too late.

Bees   I don't finish with you yet – forget about the four hundred pounds that you throw away, nothing can bring that back. I want to see how good you is, what do we do next?

Tecee   I don't know. I am trying to be serious with you. As far as I can see everybody else that use this building use it for better reason than us, all of them either talk about love or hate and all we talk about is pool, so we must either join them or leave them.

Bees   And what better way to do it in the future than over a game of pool.

Tecee   Why don't we go back to night school?

Bees   What, you idiot – I hate school. School never do anything for me. Look at this bright and pretty place, we painted it ourselves and with the luck of fortune we make enough money from pool to buy booze that we make a profit from, the squatters them like us, they all by our booze and another pool table will be here any day now – and you are telling me about school! I will stay here and play pool.

Tecee   Yes, and you will win too. Me I am going back to school.

Bees   So tell me something, do you really know what you are doing?

Tecee   Yes, the school, the fast cars, the life. Thinking seriously about money is a serious fact of life just like Moses' law, and find a life that is good for myself and family and so to be free from the aftermath. The wind is steady among the boats and no way would I be crucified grinding stones and milling corn and righteousness should be found among all the people, and let the four quarters find its true self in the 1980s.

Bees   You take on the world on your shoulders.

Tecee   That's what you think. I changed me ways, is education for me, in the eighties.

Bees   I must admit you give me a double shock.

Tecee   Man, don't be shocked.

Bees   And anyway, where are you going to get money from to keep your family while you're at school?

Tecee   But I must find some other big story to tell them other than money story.

Bees   Boy, you are bringing a permanent hate to my heart.

Tecee   Well, I could never hate you, Bees.

Bees   I want nothing more to do with you now that I find out the truth.

Tecee   I know you wouldn't get over it, when I tell you the truth and nothing but the truth.

Bees   Well, I never would believe that you'd turn so stupid about Jesus and school – everybody will remember the day you throw away four hundred pounds.

Tecee   No, man, most of it did belong to you.

Bees   Forget my share.

Bees   So what kind of school you intend going to? But we never hear about no Jesus school, boy what a long raas day. Four hundred pound, four hundred years, Jesus and now school and night don't look like it's coming down for now. Man, when are you going – which school is it?

Tecee   I don't know yet, I thinking 'bout it – because I hope to go full time when I passed me examination.

Bees   I's thinking about life from all different angles, that's why I is trying my luck at pool and nobody can beat us when we're on form – we have play some nice game together in the past. I feel seh I was going to enjoy the folks that use this building, and some of them have plenty of money in the bank – and quite a few of them like playing pool with me for money. I am going to continue to be involved with the future this of this very building. Mind you, I don't feel seh any school can teach a man like you anything.

Tecee   A change you a try to change me mind or what?

Bees   No, man, if you want to go to school you will go.

Tecee   Man, it seems like I don't have nothing to say – a lot of things is happening and I don't know anything about it so I'm thinking what's wrong with me and if other Black people is like me. Sometimes it seems to me like I alone is a individual in circumstances like these, I follow too much of those fuck-up Black people in the past.

Bees   But why take all this fuckry out on a game of pool? – that we should have win, so you should have not gone in there in the first place and pretend you was enjoying yourself all the time.

Tecee   Yes and I love everybody when I was enjoying myself, but now I hate some of their them ideas and lifestyle.

Bees   You sure seh Jesus talk to you today? Mind a pressure your under man.

Tecee   I under no pressure, I want a better life than a game of chance.

Bees   So does everybody.

Tecee   I don't want to be in any contention with you about other people.

Bees   You have gone to church today and you could have gone to school next week and we could have win a game of pool. Man, be reasonable.

Tecee   When Jesus a talk to you there is no stronger force, that's why I don't know what to tell you. As far as I can see everybody else that use this building use it for better reason than us, all of them either talk about love or hate and all we talk about is pool, so we must either join them or leave them.

Bees   So you 'fraid to tell them 'bout Jesus.

Tecee   You are mad man, you don't like Jesus, He could do a lot for you.

Bees   Just listen to yourself and listen to what you're saying about Jesus.

Tecee   You want to go and hear a man can talk about Jesus. The trouble with you is you don't know whether a man is sad or happy.

Bees   That is because you are like a steam engine without a driver, you must stop and take a look at yourself and drive your own steam engine, control it at each station so that any times station master ask you question you know the right answer.

Tecee   I never is a steam engine, I is the mighty captain of my ship, my children must have food in the future.

Bees   Don't start thinking that your intention is better than mine. I play pool and win money to buy clothes and food for my woman and children, I almost feel seh you're wicked to me picany them.

Tecee   I can't talk a raas. A what you a blame me for? I stop gamble, that's all,

Bees   You can't stop gamble, not unless every race-horse drop dead.

Tecee   You're just hurt about the game.

Bees   Maybe I didn't know you before today.

Tecee   Well, I'm sure you did know me once.

Bees   But how comes you just change suddenly?

Tecee   There is no answer.

Bees   You definitely want to do something else?

Tecee   Man, I am doing something else.

Bees   I feel there is no change for me except to follow the road that is already cut out for me. I sure seh Jesus talk to every Black man, so what your feeling is only half of the problem.

Tecee   Music, music. I want the heart of a man like myself to find peace.

Bees   I want to understand you, but I can't.

Tecee   It seems to me that your outside have gone in your inside and your inside is on the outside, so therefore is mountaintop you are headed for.

Bees   I want to do good, but love is hard to carry about in your heart for people who you feel don't love you. I feel all you are doing is repeating yourself like some of our older generation who came here before us. You can't go on the street or in a building like this and tell white people that you love them. Brother, true to God I am not with you, I don't see what I can do except to preach hate against white people and every Black man should be doing that. If there was such a thing as a good job available for me I know I would go out and find it.

Tecee   I feel seh, God might get together with the Imperial Chemical Industry to find a dye that would make everybody the same colour, but I know it will never happen.

Bees   But right now is not a colour pressure a bother me, I have two different kind of problems, life itself is coming down on top of my head and the system is showing no mercy for my children. It seems to me like every Black man lose their direction in this country when they get older and it is a waste of time blaming slavery.

Tecee   Honestly, I really don't want to stop playing pool but the money that we get from pool is a false energy for me, our homes are not safe from the bailiffs.

Bees   Listen, take it easy, we all good pool players, there is no crime in that – we spend a lot of money and time in the past learning to play the game, you can play pool and do lots of other things as well.

Tecee   What else can I do around here?

Bees   Man, I say let's go and talk to some of those people that work for the council and with any luck you don't have to go to school.

Tecee   Man, for them to listen to us we would have to go on the street and cause a lot of trouble and there is not such a thing as good troubles – and anyway, we have done all that before, that's why we are in this building.

Bees   Well, I must admit that I've never seen this side of you before.

Tecee   Yes, brother, Jesus was a strong man in my heart over that game of pool that I lost. I don't want to be all love and friendship with white people, and as soon as we get older they become our enemies.

Bees   Boy, I reading you, I know 'bout some of the pressure you are talking about. Yes, young and happy and old and happy is two different feelings

Tecee   Brother, make we take a good look at the world and see and feel how serious it is because a good heart worth keeping good. You see the white man a go in everything we do, so we must find another way to live with him before we are too old.

Bees   But it's not many of those white people try to understand us, sometimes all of them totally forget about us. Alright, alright, what are we going to do about this place?

Tecee   It wasn't I was in the first place.

Bees   What are you going to tell the squatters about you dropping out?

Tecee   I am going to tell them that I'm going back to school.

Bees   So what kind of examination is that you said you have to take?

Tecee   I have to do some kind of test, something like 'O' levels and a panel of people a ask you questions.

Bees   That shouldn't be too hard for you.

Tecee   Yes, I feel confident. I hope, if God spare my life – well, I want to be architect one day.

Bees   You should not have done this to me.

Tecee   I wish you was leaving this place with me then I wouldn't have to feel so sorry about it.

Bees   Don't feel sorry for me just let's forget it. I have worse happen to me in the past – I am staying here until the building fall down. How much money is in the kitty?

Tecee   I don't know, I never count it, it's in the money box where we always hide it. (**Bees** *reaches under the table and takes out a box which is taped under the top, then sits on the table and counts the money, which is eighty pounds in notes and six pounds in change.*)

Bees   Okay This place is now my responsibility.

Tecee   Fair enough.

Bees   Okay We got eighty-six pounds, I am going to be reasonable with you.

Tecee   Thanks.

Bees   I'm going to give you forty, I won't share the silver with you. (*He gives* **Tecee** *money.*)

Tecee   Thanks, bra. So I might as well collect my shirt off the postal orders.

Bees   So what's wrong with you? You didn't hear I say I bet extra on the side that you would sink the black after you sink the red.

Tecee   Is not pool I am talking about – I am talking about the postal orders them that we buy together at the post office.

Bees   So you think that it's the four hundred pounds that a drive me mad? But wait a minute, look how many times we lost games for two and three hundred pounds at a time.

Tecee   You bet £1,000 postal orders on one game of pool?

Bees   Yes and we be rich now if you didn't fuck it up.

Tecee   And it's the red shirt of Liverpool moving forward Hughes, Toshack, Dalglish, all units, all units, this house.

Bees   I know what that means, I am going to protect myself. (*He runs for door,* **Tecee** *gets there before him.*) Battlestations, battlestations, to raas. (*He runs back to the table and grabs the whiskey bottle.*)

Tecee   Me money, me head, the fever, me heart. (*He is clutching his chest while falling to floor.*)

Bees   No, Tecee, no, Tecee. (*He puts bottle back on table.*) I sorry, I sorry. (*He moves towards* **Tecee**, *trying to get him on his feet.*) I sorry, I sorry, there is still £500 left.

Tecee (*waking up on his feet*)   I know you was a good friend. (*They break into hysterical laughter and start wrestling with each other; they continue until they almost run out of breath, then they start slapping and holding each other.*)

Bees   Well, I hope you do well at school.

Tecee   I will.

Bees   I feel different now that I am on my own, underneath it all you're a good friend.

Tecee   Fancy a game of pool?

Bees   No, I would rather play darts.

Tecee   Darts! Let's toss for it.

Bees   You want to drink? (**Bees** *picks up coin from table.*) Okay, call.

Tecee   Heads.

Blackout.

No Soldiers in St Paul's

Characters

Mary, *age twenty-three to twenty-five, dressed in mini-skirt and shirt*
Alvin, *age twenty-six to twenty-nine, dressed in crumpled suit with tie undone,*
 pork-pie hat
Byron, *age twenty-five to twenty-seven, dressed in jeans and jacket*
Hazel, *age twenty-six to twenty-nine, dressed in mini-skirt and suede or leather jacket,*
tall boots
Dickie, *age twenty-eight to thirty-one, smartly best in mohair suit, bracelet and flashy*
gold watch

All characters are Jamaican.

Mary *sits on bed with boots on and fully dressed, eating sandwich, drinking coffee, reading the* Daily Mirror *and listening to the wireless.*

'And now that great little champion from Liverpool with his first hit, Jimmy Osmond and "Long-Haired Lover from Liverpool". The little man that the thirteen- and fourteen-year-old girls are crazy about. Here goes, "Long-Haired Lover from Liverpool".'

Music plays for one minute.

Slow footsteps coming up the staircase.

Mary *turns wireless down, puts newspaper on chair, sits on bed and continues eating sandwich and drinking coffee.*

Enter **Alvin**, *very tired out gambling all night. Tie undone, shirt hanging out of his trousers. He turns wireless off, and turns straight to racing page of newspaper.*

Mary *finishes eating.*

She puts away the cup and stands looking at **Alvin** *very angry.*

Mary   You are as good as dead you send me out to work yet I can't afford a pair of stockings. Half the time we don't have anything to eat. You take any more money that I work for to the gambling house, why you bother to come home I don't know. Yes your holiday is over, the gambling house you can have all of you from now on. I am not living with you for another day, the million pound that you are going to make you can keep it for yourself and the gambling house. I am going to have a good time like anyone else. Yes, Lord, the bag of money that you promised Alvin he can keep it for himself. I don't want any of it. I can never understand why you are so lazy. Four years I lived with you and I still don't know you, you better go and register with the prison authority because there is no judge in England who would allow you to stand trial in their court house. I swear to God the judge would hang you there and then – you bastard.

Alvin   Did I ask you to come and live with me?

Mary   No but you make sure that you beat all my senses out of me so I didn't know what I was doing.

Alvin   I think you better pack your clothes and leave.

Mary (*moves to chair*)   I should leave, the rent book is in my name, your memory seems to be getting shorter and shorter every day. Nobody in their right mind would rent you anywhere to live. You don't remember what the landlord said to you about people who don't have a regular job. I must have been mad to live with you. I am having another man in the house before the week's finished.

Alvin   Yes I know you will always be a tramp.

Mary   I know I am a tramp, that's why a tramp have no right to live with a decent citizen like you. Two days ago the vice squad follow me all over St Paul's. Only God in Heaven knows what people's thinking. I have never done anything wrong in

England except go to work. My brother is going to kill you, people been telling him how you beat me up every day for money to take to the gambling house.

Alvin   What else could you do except go to work, don't let me lose my temper. I lose all my money last night. (*He starts to empty his pockets for money – he finds approx. 15s–18s.*)

Mary   You better listen to what I'm saying to you this morning because you'll be living on your own as from tomorrow. I'm sure you'll enjoy doing your own washing and cooking, you useless sex maniac. (**Alvin** *turns wireless up to full volume –* **Mary** *panics and backs towards the wall.* **Alvin** *slowly starts moving towards her. Knock at the door – enter* **Byron**.) I didn't hear anybody say come in.

Byron   What?

Mary   Oh Jesus Christ, what is this?

Byron   Boy, it's like I am just coming from Bridewell Magistrates Court, the man gets nine months.

Alvin   What – who get nine months?

Byron   So you didn't remember that they arrest Calvin down the gambling house.

Mary   Bloody good. It will be you next. (*Rushing out, slamming door.*)

Alvin *turns wireless off.*

Alvin   Boy, it's like I did forget about his trial this morning.

Byron   I'm hungry, man, I could do with something to eat.

Alvin   I don't know if any food is in the kitchen, I will go and have a look in a minute. I had a bad night last night, I lose all my money.

Byron   Well, when I left you were winning – so who win up the money last night?

Alvin   I don't know, Dickie win all the money again.

Byron   That Dickie been lucky these past few weeks how come he's so lucky. Is only about two days ago the man win about £50 just like that.

Alvin   That's right Dickie don't have to worry about going to work, because he always win other people's money. So how did Calvin take his sentence? Did his woman turn up at the trial?

Byron   Yes, man, she tell the vice squad that he have drugs in his house. Any woman who cause me to go to prison I would surely kill them to raasclath. After she finish giving evidence against him and after they take him downstairs to the prison cells she start crying in the courthouse saying she's sorry while she sits down arms in arms with Ralph so now he's in prison knowing that Ralph's sleeping in his bed every night. Boy, me sure when Calvin come out of prison he bound to kill both of them. That's the reason I don't have a woman in my house living with me. I don't know women. Your woman was angry a while ago when I came in.

Alvin No, she's not feeling too good this morning but you know Mary, she'll be alright.

Byron Boy, you're very lucky to have such a good woman like Mary, I really like her. Since she's been living with you she haven't looked at another man. Maybe I could find a woman like Mary then perhaps I would live with one of them but I can't see that happening in my lifetime.

Knock at door. **Byron** *goes and opens door.*

Hazel (*at door*) Hello, Byron, Byron is Mary at home?

Byron No it's just me and Alvin here at the moment.

Alvin Come in, Hazel, Mary will be back in a minute.

Hazel Oh then I will wait – she asked me to come round today since it's the New Year and all that. She was quite depressed last night – is she feeling sick?

Alvin No nothing ain't wrong with her, she's all right – have a seat, Hazel.

Byron Well, Hazel, have you a little present in your purse for me but, Hazel, you must be very rich. Since the day I know you you been saving up your money, your mattress must be as hard as the Rock of Gibraltar with £10 notes. Look, Hazel, I am single man so why don't you let me take care of you and your £10 notes. I could make a nice woman like you very happy. It was only last night I was thinking I could be a poet just for you. (*He takes a piece of paper from his pocket. He reads from paper.*) I am a river so please come and wash in my pure river water.

Hazel You always full of shit, you're the last man I would have anything to do with, an way you're not even a man. I can't think of any woman in St Paul's who'd have anything to do with you, oh piss off and don't bother me.

Alvin Talk proper romance to the woman, man. Make she know what kind of man you is. Make she know what she's missing.

Byron I wouldn't waste my time, me can get better woman than she.

Hazel Jesus Christ, listen to the half-wit, you're not even a mouse.

Alvin *starts laughing.*

Byron I am the only one who's going to last one day.

Knock at door.

Alvin I wonder who that is – come in.

Enter **Dickie**.

Alvin Wait – what's happening, Dickie, I didn't expect to see you so early.

Dickie Man, it's like I am just coming from the Jew tailor down the road. What's happening, Hazel?

He slaps her on the shoulder.

Gal, you're getting nice and nicer every day. Byron, you're not working.

Byron   No, man, I am on the ten to six shift – remember I am working on the motorway.

Hazel   Dickie, come sit beside me and let me see what's in your pocket. When you visit the Jew tailor's, things must be looking good in your pockets.

Dickie *sits beside* **Hazel**.

Alvin   Hazel, why don't you two get married – that would give me a chance to buy a new suit.

Byron   You think Dickie's a fool, he wouldn't marry somebody like Hazel.

Hazel   Shut up before I piss all over you.

Everybody laughs.

Dickie   You two always make me laugh when I come here.

Alvin   So, Dickie, Byron just tell me that they give Calvin nine months.

Dickie   Yes, man, I know they were talking about it down the gambling house just before I left. I'm not sure if I was sorry for him – did you know it was his woman who lock him up?

Hazel   But it's not the first time his white woman call the police to arrest him.

Alvin   Boy, it's like I don't know what to say but Calvin is not a fool.

Hazel   Well, it's a Black man from the same district in Jamaica tell Calvin white woman to lock him up.

Byron   I feel sorry for Calvin. His woman tell the police that he have drugs in the house but when they search his house they didn't find any drugs. You know that little penknife he walks with in his pocket is ph'ensic test the police do on the knife – anyway I never trust white people especially the rasclath police. The police say they believe the knife was used for cutting up cannabis.

Dickie   I talked to Calvin a hundred times, I tell him his woman was no good, but he never listen to me.

Hazel   But I don't see what these Black men see in these white women. If Calvin was living with a Black woman she would never lock him up. White women will always lock them up. Me know a nice Black gal who really likes him and all he do is beat her up and take her money to buy pretty drawers for his white woman – the judges should give him twenty years.

Alvin   Me and him move quite nice together – I think I still owe him £20.

Dickie   I don't say I won't play about with a white woman – I went to bed with a few of them but no, sir, I will never live with any white woman.

Byron   You're right, Dickie, just imagine Calvin is in jail while another Black man is sleeping in his bed and riding his woman every night. Yes, my brothers, I don't want no white woman. Some of the Black men is twice as wicked as white people once they start smelling white woman drawers.

Hazel   Oh piss off, Byron – when people are having a serious discussion.

Alvin   Byron, Hazel is really giving you hell today.

Byron   A love she love me, man.

Hazel   Did you know the rat offer me his pay packet to go to bed with him – I wouldn't even let him smell me drawers.

Everybody laughs.

Byron   You're only bragging because Dickie's here. Just listen to her talking about Calvin and white woman – she only fucks with white men.

Alvin   Oh cut out all this white and Black business. Can't we talk about something that it is more sensible than that – it's a free country, she can live with anybody she wants to live with – white or Black.

Hazel   Jesus Christ, I will glad for the day when you find a woman.

Dickie   Is one thing I know dis is a free country and I am a thinking man.

Alvin   Anyway, Hazel you seen Chris recently?

Hazel   Yes we almost live together now.

Alvin   Well, tell him I want to see him.

Hazel   Okay, I'll bring him around tomorrow evening.

Alvin   Nice and we could have a smoke and a drink – together.

Dickie   But, Hazel, is a long time now you've been sleeping with Chris.

Hazel   Well, I like him and he take me out to some very nice places.

Alvin   You see that's what I mean – poor Byron will never have a chance to take you to bed because you know you like expensive things.

Dickie   You can say that again, boy – one day me was up Clifton on the Downs, I couldn't believe me eyes, me see Hazel a ride horse with a white man, they just gallop past me. But, Hazel, where do you meet those kinda white men because nobody ever see those kind of rich white people in St Paul's.

Hazel   From me come to England me get on with white people – would love to live with a Black man but they can't give me the kind of expensive things I want and anyway we all love to have expensive things from white people. I feel sorry for all those Black people who leave the West Indies and come here to become slaves.

Dickie   Well, Hazel, gal, I wish you luck if you find white men who's willing to keep you that's good.

Alvin   Hazel, what kind of car Chris got now?

Hazel   E-Type Jag.

Byron   Jesus Christ, E-Type Jag, boy, I'll never stop doing the pools. Man, me read last week where a Black man wins £50,000 on the pools – I think it was Littlewoods. Do you still do the pools, Alvin?

Alvin   You think I have money to throw away – the gambling house takes all the money I got.

Dickie   Me have five draws last week – it's sure to come up one day.

Bryon   Hey, Dickie, let's play a few hands of cards, man.

Dickie   You have any money? Because when you finish buying pussy out of the little money you earn on the motorway nothing ain't left out of it to play cards with. Anyway you playing, Alvin?

Alvin   Yes, man.

Hazel   But, Alvin, Mary taking a long time to come back, where is she?

Alvin   She's mad, she didn't say where she's going.

Dickie   Hazel, why don't you go and cook us something to eat?

Hazel   Boy, me don't know how to cook these days, I only eat in restaurants.

Byron*'s shuffling cards.*

Byron   Maybe Hazel would like to have a game of cards with us since she is so rich.

Dickie   Shut your rassclath mouth, Bryon – you ever see me gambling with woman. It seems like you don't know that a woman's place doesn't belong in gambling. (*Gets money from his pocket.*) Hazel, see 30s. here go and buy us some food down the road and cook us some nice beef soup.

Hazel   Well, that's alright I can cook that sort of thing but 30s. can't buy anything, every time I go to the shop I spend £10 or more – anyway I've got some money.

Byron   You better off now playing cards, Hazel, and anyway I haven't eaten since yesterday.

Hazel   Oh God he never gives up.

Dickie   Thanks, Hazel, you're a good sport.

He gives **Hazel** *money – exit* **Hazel**. **Dickie** *takes cannabis from his pocket and cigarette papers.*

Dickie   I like Hazel very much that since she like rassclath white men too much. Boy, me sure she been to bed with a million of them since she come to England. I don't want to play cards, I just feel like having a good smoke. Alvin, why do you want Hazel to bring Chris round here to see you?

Alvin   Man, I want to discuss some business with him about the money.

Dickie   Man, you are living dangerously, having white people in your house.

Byron   No, man, Chris is alright.

Dickie   Byron, you a man have no sense at all where people stalk. Why don't you shut up and go and lock yourself in the madhouse up in Fish Ponds?

Byron   Why everybody thinks I don't have no sense, you all seems to forget that I am a carpenter. You so clever why don't you have a trade?

Alvin starts reading newspaper.

Dickie   What I want a trade for? You think I want to be a idiot like you – like you don't see the kind of suits I wear. Is £40 a time I pay for my suits.

Byron   I can't afford £40 suits – is work I work for my money. I don't sell drugs or live off woman.

Dickie   You want to go and tell the vice squad that I am selling drugs and living off woman – have I ever sell you drugs? The cannabis you sitting down there smoking you paying any money for it? Why every time I come to this house this bloodcloth guy is here. All you do with your money is buy woman with it. Woman have to pay me to go to bed with them. This is the last time I am going to give you a smoke. Any time the vice squad lock me up I am going to chop you up the same way they chopped up old fowl in Jamaica. Is Black men like you to lock up other Black people.

Byron   Alvin, tell your friend that I keep drugs in my house for different people and I never lock anybody up. Boy, the things I have got to put up with. All I said was that Chris was a nice fella. Alvin, did I do the guy anything?

Alvin   Quiet yourself, man, and smoke up the ganja.

Dickie   You think I would trust you is because you don't know I see you talking to the vice squad the other night because I don't say anything.

Byron stands up.

Byron   Jesus Christ, what but look at my troubles.

Dickie   What you standing up for? What are you going to do – is fight you want to fight. As far as you concerned I am Sonny Liston to you.

Alvin   Nobody no bother mash up the house you know.

Byron   I should tell the vice squad man about you, Alvin, please listen to me, man.

Alvin   I am listening, say what you want to say, man.

Byron   You, see how people can get themselves into trouble for their own good is the vice squad man stop me in the street and asking me if I know Dickie but I know the man was making a fool of me because I know that is the vice squad man see me and Dickie walking about the street together. So I tell the vice squad man that I don't know nobody called Dickie. I tell the man since I come to England I haven't stopped working yet and it is five years now me still working for the same firm and me not a idiot, I am a tradesman. He's the same vice squad man we saw in the pub the other night, wearing a ginger-coloured wig. Is the same man asked me where Alvin get his money from to go gambling so often. Remember I tell you about it?

Alvin *leaps to his feet.*

Alvin   You never tell me they was asking about me.

Dickie   Almighty God, the police know everything you are doing. They must have been watching you for the last three months.

Alvin   Man, don't worry, I am not doing anything wrong.

Byron   I sorry, man, if I didn't tell you – I must forget.

Alvin   Don't worry, Byron boy, let them piss off.

Dickie   You see what I mean, is the same thing I was saying before this fool Byron start bothering me. As soon as white people in the house the vice squad is going to break the door down and the next thing you know we will end up in jail to rassclath.

Alvin   It's alright, man, Chris is not a beatnik, is only when the police see beatniks start visiting your house the vice squad start thinking about drugs.

Dickie   But what happen, man, when Chris start bringing his friends to visit you? As soon as the vice squad see white people anywhere near your house they will break the door down. They go as far as raiding Norman House last Sunday.

Alvin   No, man, it's alright the beatniks are the only type of white people who walks about the street in groups of twos and threes. The vice squad did not know Black people smoke ganja until the beatnik start coming around St Paul's trying to buy drugs.

Dickie   What do you mean, the beatniks trying to buy drugs. Some Black men only sell drugs to beatniks because the beatniks are the only ones who got any money to spare. They so foolish they pay £10 for a couple of smokes. Now, if I was one of the Black man in St Paul's selling drugs to beatniks them you would have to pay £100 or more an ounce for my ganja.

Byron   No, man, that would not be right, it would be too expensive.

Dickie   Shut your rass mouth, you don't see how much money whiskies and Guinnesses cost these days. Those Black men is taking a long time to learn their lesson. They want to go to school and let the teacher beat fuck out of them. These Black men who's selling drugs don't realise that good ganja is too good for white people. Black men should buy some of the tea that they have in the supermarket that they imported from India where the people are dropping dead with hunger and hard work, picking tea to send to England for the tea-break they have in the sugar refineries and use some of the same sugar that they imported from Jamaica. Sprinkle a little sugar over a large amount of tea from India, roast the two together in a deep saucepan and sell it to a type of beatnik like the Rolling Stones. The big time beatniks them who use scissors to cut up a brand new pair of jeans and patch them, wear them down King's Road and Carnaby Street and call the jeans fashions, while half the population of India is writing letters to Oxfam every week, begging for old jeans or any other old clothes. All the big time beatniks them do is thief Black people music, television and call it pop and the *Sunday Times* is there to review pop every fucking Sunday.

Byron   A man should never smoke ganja with white people. I never can understand white people when they are talking together.

Dickie   I spent all of last week looking for a job and I get a letter this morning saying I've got one, that's the reason I come round to see you so soon. I am leaving St Paul's. The whole district is full of police since I'm going to start this job next week, so I send my woman to look for a flat miles away from St Paul's. I think I better stop smoking ganja, boy, it's like if I would go to jail it would kill me. I am going to hide myself among white people up in Clifton, there is too many Black informers and police walking about St Paul's for my liking.

Byron   From the day I come to live in St Paul's I want to move. Boy I really try to get a room somewhere else but I can't find one. When the time comes for me to receive my old age pension St Paul's is where the postman is going to deliver my register letter.

Dickie *moves across to* **Alvin***, grabs newspaper from him.*

Dickie   Alvin, you should not spend all your time reading horse-racing, you should read the other pages, at least you would find out how much money to people spend on whiskies and Guinnesses in England.

Alvin   Yeah, man, it's alright, give me back the paper.

Dickie *gives him paper.* **Alvin** *goes straight back to racing page.*

Dickie   Alvin, let Mary go and look for a flat, man, let we move from St Paul's.

Alvin   I am not moving, man, what am I doing wrong. I only have a smoke now and then and anyway I'm going to stop smoking ganja – well at least for a while anyway.

Byron   Man, it's like I can't stop smoking ganja. I work hard for my money and that is all the comfort I get out of life.

Alvin   When Hazel come back I am going to tell her not to bother to bring Chris round to see me.

Dickie   But me didn't understand why you want Chris to come here in the first place. You mark my word as soon as people start coming in the house, the vice squad will raid the house.

Byron   Boy, I don't think Hazel would understand why you don't want Chris to come here.

Dickie   Why are you worried about Hazel? Don't you see if she have the white man supporting her, you want to start worrying about your own problems.

Byron   I mean these people are really taking liberties with us, I only hope nobody or police don't start bothering me because as soon as I leave here today I am going to buy a hatchet.

Dickie   Is only my woman I am worried about although I fool about with other women and do my little gambling, and have a smoke of ganja with the boys now and then but as soon as I get home I become a very serious man because my woman is my number one, boy, she's the only thing I got in the world.

Byron   Yes, man, I like the way you and your woman move together. Remember the time when she come looking for you down the gambling house and you beat her up, well everybody said she was going to leave you and that she was too good for you but me know you look after your woman with a loving.

Dickie   Boy, is like me and she have a little argument this morning, man, is like I'm getting tired of beating the woman. Sometime I feel like leaving her and start all over again but I can't leave her because I really miss her if I go in the house and don't see her.

Byron   Boy, I know she's one of the strongest Black woman in the world because me see you throw licks for over her body and she come back at you stronger than Cassius Clay and Frazier put together but she did put you in the hospital couple of years ago because in those days you was a good boy and you never used to gamble you used to just stand around and watch other people gamble.

Dickie   Alvin, listen to this story, man.

Alvin   Yes, man, I am listening.

Dickie   Well, I used to fool around with a white girl. You want to hear how I catch her. Anyway I tell you how I catch up afterwards. Well, me round my house one day with this white girl, the last person I expect to see was my woman. She just walk in the room and start beating this white girl and what hurt me is money I am trying to hustle from the white girl. All I said to the woman is that she should control her temper. The next thing I know is me and this white girl in the same ambulance going to hospital. Is the electric light iron she use across my head. Man, me lay in hospital with my whole body numb and she come to visit me in the hospital and start crying her eyes out saying she sorry she hit me with the electric iron. Man, me start crying too but the only reason I was crying is because I was too weak to get up out of the hospital bed to beat her. Boy, the other day me and she fight and she hit me with the right hook and me have to stop and ask her if she's a man.

Alvin   Man, whether I like it or not it look like I have to go to the labour exchange for a job.

He puts newspaper down and stands up.

It's four months now I get laid off work and I gamble out the little money that Mary have save up. Where am I going to get money from? I am too nervous to sell ganja, I will have to go to get a job or the vice squad is going to put me in the madhouse. Now if I go on the street and start fighting one of them vice squad they bound to send me to prison.

Byron   Alvin, be careful, man, because I wouldn't like anything to happen to you because me know you are a violent man. Man, that's why I don't go anywhere. The only place I go when I finish work is down the gambling house or I come up here to have a smoke with you, that's why I can't understand how sometimes you and some of the boys go all the way down town for a drink. Man, since the day I come and live in this town I don't go nowhere for a drink except St Paul's. Alvin, when I see you going down town all by yourself I get worried I think them white people might beat you up. Alvin, tell me something why white people don't like us? Man, what do they think is wrong with us because the white people them that I work with they like me and I like them so why the other white people don't like us? Boy, I can't understand it.

Alvin   Man, there is nothing to understand about white people.

Dickie   Boy, is a long time now I know these people don't like Black people. Man I feel good the other night watching television. I see a Black man give a white man a beating. The Black man knock him right out in the third round. Man, I said to my woman, now you see how white people weak. They can't fight like a Black man.

Byron   Jesus Christ, man, I nearly cry last week. I was watching sport on BBC, I think it was on a Saturday. You want to see the Black man let the white man nearly beat him to death. The referee had to stop the fight. Boy, I really feel ashamed.

Alvin   But why is the vice squad asking about me? The only reason the vice squad could know my name is because I went and signed on down the labour exchange a couple of weeks ago but I haven't gone back to the labour exchange. Boy, I don't think I am going back to the labour exchange. Is like the vice squad was waiting to know who I was. Now where am I going to find a job? Where am I going to find a job? If I don't go to the labour exchange maybe Chris could get me a job but I can't have white people in the house. The vice squad is only going to break the door down. Boy, this kind of pressure is going to kill me.

Dickie   Man, I hold some pressure in this town, this country's too much for my liking. You want to see me not long ago, I went down the assistance board to ask them if I could have some money. You want to hear some of the questions the man behind the counter was asking me? He ask me the same kind of question just like if he were the vice squad man – that's the time I know me and my woman don't belong in this country, but I am not leaving England. The kind of white people that work in the assistance board is the same type you find drinking half a bitter in the pub every night and telling the same dirty jokes to one another that they tell them the night before. Because they see the Black man as Sambo – they expect you to laugh at Sambo's joke. Those kind of white people is just as wicked to their own white people as they are to Black people. Five years ago they make you believe that any white man with long hair was worse than a Black man but I'll say it again, I'm not leaving England.

Byron   My mother and father drop dead the same time in Jamaica because bulldozer run over them in the cane fields, me sell the house and the little piece of land that they left and bury them. A month after that I came to England, no government did not help me to come to England, so no government is going to tell me to leave. Is the white English man come all the way to Jamaica to recruit me to work on the buses but

I didn't pay him no mind. I pay my own fare to come to England. I am never going to go to the labour exchange or the rassclath assistance board. I am working hard for my money so I can buy pussy and enjoy myself, if I did not smoke ganja the weather would kill me – I don't want anything from any white man.

Alvin   Boy, me can't believe that the vice squad is looking for me. What am I going to do? I can't get a job, I might as well keep beating the woman and send her out to work, she will have to earn the money to keep us one way or the other. I think I better go out and look for Mary because I don't know where she's gone.

Dickie   Man, let we leave the rassclath district and find somewhere else to live. Man, I can lend you some money.

Byron   Alvin, you know you can have anything at all that belongs to me and I have got a few pounds saved.

Alvin   How the rassclath money going to help me when the vice squad looking for me. Man, I am going out to look for my woman and what the rassclath happen to Hazel with the shopping.

Exit **Alvin**.

Byron   Take it easy, brother, watch out for the vice squad. Is one thing I know, if them rassclath vice squad carry Alvin to a jail they will have to jail me to because you and him is my best friend. What's wrong with these vice squad white people, tell me what are we doing wrong?

Dickie   We're not doing anything wrong, man, the vice squad think they know everything about us and they can't understand why we should be happy and laughing at each other because since time began the white people got everything they wanted plus what they rob from all the other poor people. Man, when you read books you will see that the English vice squad have police stations all over the world and they are still not happy – they don't even talk to each other except when they want something, boy, life is really funny, yet we have never own anything and we are twice as happy as the vice squad, don't you ever wonder why they call us sunshine? Me sure me will never get rich and me know they will never like Black people. I stop wasting my time hating white people a long time ago, why bother to hate them – what good is it. Is one thing I know, if any of them bother me me will just chop them up bloodcloth, rassclath I am not going to bother to move to Clifton, because anywhere we go is going to be the same vice squad following us all over their fucking place.

Byfon   Man, is a few years back me realise that we are Black and they are white but is one thing I know, every vice squad will have to go to hell, because me can't see white people and Black people sitting side-by-side in heaven, and God isn't going to let them make drug slaves of us again.

Dickie   You think it's a joke but it's a long time me know these white people is wasting their time going to church to pray, that's why I like my woman because she go to the library and borrow books and sometime when I'm in the house and don't have anything better to do me start reading some of the books but me not tell anybody that we read book. You want to read some of the bad things them white people do to Black people. The way those Black people suffer they must be safe in heaven by now and I know there is only one heaven, so God will have to throw the white man out of heaven or there will be no peace.

Byron   It takes me ten years in England for me to realise how much I hate our woman Bible-teacher when I was going to school, she was as Black as the ace of spades in hell, man, she teach us all the good things about the Bible and before the Bible lesson finish she would tell you all about World War I. She spirit was an expert on the different guns that the Germans use on the English in World War II. Man she make you believe that God, war and the English is your only way of life, then she would finish by telling you why our mothers and fathers are very wicked to let five of us kids sleep in the same bed at night, then out she would come with the chart of the Black Hole of Calcutta and show you what happen to the English soldiers because the Indians put all of them in one room and they died because of lack of oxygen by then you're half asleep in the boiling hot classroom.

Dickie   I bet you never tell you anything about the English general who shoot down innocent women and children in the park.

Byron   No, sir, I don't know anything about that. Somebody tell me the other day that Hazel commit sodomy with one of those white girls from up Clifton.

Dickie   You mean lesbian, well me not sure about that but if Hazel make love to one of those white girls she would do it for money and you can't blame Black people for making money from all sorts of sins in this country. Sometime we go to parties where you see two women making love.

Byron   Well, didn't you feel sick and vomit?

Dickie   No, man, that don't bother me. There's a lot of things me see in this country well you know like how we have blues dance party and all we do is smoke a ganja joint and dance to a few reggae records, well sometimes when some of these white people are having parties man and man and woman and woman is making love in the same room – that is what white people called kinky.

Byron   Man, can't believe what people do that sort of thing. Me know six of them boys make love to the same woman in less than one hour but five of them line up outside the door so there's only one man in the room with the woman.

Enter **Mary**.

Mary   Hello, Dickie, you still here, Byron?

Byron   Yes, man.

Dickie   But Alvin left a while ago to look for you – did he find you?

Mary   No, he will never find me, I am leaving him for good and if he lay a finger on me I am calling the police. Oh God I can't stand him or this place no more, all he do with the money I work for in the factory is take it to the gambling house and give it to those good-for-nothing niggers hanging about the fucking streets. Well, what's the future in it for me – look at Hazel she's happy and yet she never done a day's work in her life, and she find lots of men to take her to the best places in town.

Byron   But Hazel only go out with white men.

Mary   Well, what's wrong with white man, I have never seen a white man beating his woman, just look at me black and blue all over.

She lifts her dress and shows her legs.

Two days ago Alvin nearly beat me to death, the next day I have to go to work with pain all over my body. Well, there's a lot of Black women living quite happy with white men and don't give me none of this shit that it's only Black men can satisfy a woman in bed. If white man can satisfy Hazel than I am sure they can satisfy me.

Byron   Well, Dickie.

Dickie   Well, Dickie what. Mary's not my woman, she's Alvin woman. Boy is like whatever I know I am keeping it to myself because since I know that I am a very serious man and with the vice squad outside watching the Black people with prison sentence hanging over their heads, what can a man say. Is one thing I know, if Mary was my woman she wouldn't talk like that about me. This room is getting too hot for me.

Enter **Hazel**.

Hazel   Sorry I take so long but there's about a hundred people stopping me in the street and was talking to me, where is hell going on in 57 – as you can see I've got no shopping. Oh God I feel sick, why Black people so stupid. Well, as you know everybody in St Paul's knows the vice squad was watching 57, well right outside the off-licence one of the vice squad man stop me, I think he's after me and he was asking how I was and what I was doing but I don't pay him no mind and then is like a whole army of them police rush into 57, it was one of the biggest raids the police ever have in St Paul's. You want to see how many of the Black people was looking at me and do you want to hear what one of them dirty rassclath nigger says me who send the vice squad to 57.

She starts crying – nobody shows any emotion.

I would not look up a Black person. I don't even know what's going on in 57 because I don't mix with Black people it doesn't mean I don't live there. We all come to England hoping we would better ourselves, it's not my fault if half of them end up in jail and the rest of them put away in the madhouse.

Mary   Oh Jesus Christ, please don't cry, Hazel, I know how you feel.

Byron   I know something like this would happen sooner or later.

Dickie   I am not saying a thing, bomboclath, give me back my 30s., Hazel.

Hazel   What you mean?

She throws money at **Dickie**.

Dickie   Nobody don't bother ask me a thing because I don't want to go to jail.

Byron   Just because you a cry, Hazel. you try to make excuses that you don't understand what Dickie's talking about.

Mary   What's going on in this rass house?

Hazel   Don't you see they don't believe me.

Dickie   Me will never trust white people or love white people as much as some people do.

Mary   So tell me something, Dickie. Is you telling Hazel that she love white people more than she loves Black people?

Byron   Is the same thing we were talking about just before she come back from the shop.

Hazel   The lot of you kiss me bomboclath. Me know why Black people don't like me, is because everything that I have got I get it off white people.

Dickie   Hazel, you can tell Byron and Mary that kind of rubbish but not me, you don't see the kind of suits I wear is over £40 a time I paid for my suits. You think white people's going to pay that kind of money for their suits? So I don't have the time to waste talking to white people on the street corner, especially the vice squad when they are sending Black people to prison. I know there's a lot of Black informers in St Paul's.

Byron   A truth, Dickie, a talk.

Mary   You two don't believe Hazel would lock up and inform on Black people, is one thing I know no rassclath man could talk to me like that.

Byron   This don't concern you, Mary.

Hazel   Look who is talking, the little dirty rassclath.

Dickie   Shut your bomboclath mouth, Hazel. Look at the dirty kind of white men you go to bed with. At least Byron don't give information to the vice squad, if me ever go to prison is for chopping up bloodclath Black people. If my woman ever mix with some Black woman I would kill her, that's why she have to stay in the house and don't go on the street corner and talk to certain Black people.

Byron   Jesus Christ, Dickie, you're so right. Some of the Black people is worse than the vice squad they just sit around and thief other Black people money and go and give it to the betting shop, while the Black women sell their pussy to the white men and give information to the vice squad.

Mary   You have no right to talk to Hazel like that, Byron.

Byron   This don't concern you, Mary, you're Alvin woman.

Alvin *rushes into the room.*

Alvin   Bomboclath, the vice squad just raid 57.

Byron   We know, man, Hazel just tell us.

Alvin   But don't you realise they carry Sonny and Ralph down the police station, more prison sentence for Black people, man I'm too shocked to talk.

Hazel   Did you say the vice squad arrest Ralph?

Alvin   Yes.

Byron   Mind you that could be a curse on Ralph because it's Ralph who cause Calvin to get nine months' prison sentence this morning.

Alvin   As for you, Mary, I am going to murder you rassclath, Lord God my own woman bring disgrace on me what did you stay home from work today. So you are giving information to the vice squad. Every Black man in St Paul's see you talking to the vice squad this morning.

Mary   You see how did Black people are stupid, Hazel, just because a white man who always stands on the corner of city road and Brighton Street stop me and was talking to me about the weather and what a lovely day it was at least he said he notice what a hard working girl I was and that I was different from the other girls in St Paul's and I was right to take the day off from work because it was the New Year, I don't care he was a nice white man.

Alvin   I know one thing if you live to see tomorrow you will never talk to a white man again, I shall murder your rassclath this Tuesday.

Byron   Mary, I'm sorry for you.

Hazel   Shut your mouth, Byron, Mary's not your equal.

Byron *rushes across to* **Hazel***.*

Byron   If you ever open your rassclath mouth to me again I am going to kick you right in your pussy, you're the first woman I made up my mind to kill. I am a big man, not one of your rassclath white man who fucking you every night. You are worse than a prostitute, and you give rassclath information to the fucking vice squad.

Hazel *spits on the floor.*

Hazel   You stinking bastard, you so dirty you smell.

She starts screaming, she attacks **Byron***.*

Hazel   I am going to prison today.

Dickie *and* **Alvin** *look on uninterested,* **Mary** *rushes between them and gets* **Byron** *away from* **Hazel***.*

Mary   Stop it, Byron, don't worry, Hazel, they think I'm giving information to the police too.

Byron   Listen, Mary, all I was going to say to you is that the same man that stand at the corner of Brighton Street and City Road it was the same man who was asking me about Alvin and Dickie.

Mary   Oh God, my rassclath head need testing.

Alvin   Don't you understand that the same vice squad man me see drag Sonny out of 57. For the last two weeks the same white man been standing on the corner watching 57, everybody in St Paul's know he's a vice squad man except my woman, the thing that really hurts me everybody knows that Sonny don't smoke ganja and now he's in jail, all because the vice squad find piece of hash on the chair he was sitting on.

Dickie   See me sitting down here smoking my ganja and I am not saying nothing, there is nowhere else for us to go at night except the gambling house. The only thing wrong that the woman who own 57 is doing is cooking food and selling it to Black people, she don't know nothing about vice squad I bet all those Black men can eat her food every day didn't tell her the vice squad was watching her house. There is too many Black informers in St Paul's, my woman could never talk to a white nan because she know I would kill her, no Black woman have any right at all to go on the street corner talking to white man. I know one thing, some man don't know how to handle their woman, from the day I was born until now I don't know any woman with any sense unless you beat some into them.

Byron   Charlie got five years for nearly beating his woman to death for talking to white men on the street.

Mary   But it's alright for Black men to go and sleep with different white women every night. I never hear any of you complaining about that. Look how many Black men in St Paul's lying with white woman, some of them even have three or four kids, you see how we women were born to suffer, Hazel.

Hazel   I'm not suffering, I am making sure I am having a good time, as long as there's been around I'll enjoy myself, here or in Jamaica.

Byron   It's different for men, Mary most of the Black man is only hustling money from the white women. As for Hazel, well she's an animal.

Hazel   Lord God, I better leave this house before I kill this half tramp, half punk.

Mary   Don't worry, Hazel. So why should you men have everything your own way?

Alvin   Shut your rassclath mouth.

*He rushes across to **Mary**.*

Byron   You can't beat the woman with all of us in the room, Alvin man.

Alvin   She will have to learn not to be so cheeky, you just wait, Miss Mary, I will finish you and your brother before long.

Dickie   I am sure the vice squad wouldn't mind having a murder in St Paul's, at least it would ease up the pressure on the prostitutes and the drug sellers. There is not a single day of peace in our lives, the woman then will have to learn to have more senses and I know there is only one way to teach a woman any sort of sense.

Hazel   Yes I know, you have to beat them, Lord give me a gun so I can shoot these mad rassclath Black people. Dickie, why don't you go home and beat your own woman?

Mary   Don't bother with these men, Hazel, because it doesn't matter what happens to me. I have no more bones left to be broken, Alvin broke every single bone in my body more than once and now he's calling me police informer, look how hard I work for the money that he takes to the gambling house.

Alvin   Shut up, before I go and buy you a packet of rubbers and put you on the street, so you have lots of news to tell the vice squad because if you don't go to work you must be a prostitute, you lazy rassclath.

Byron   Take it easy, man, this is what the vice squad want you to do, so they could arrest you for poncing, because the vice squad man was asking me if any man were visiting Mary, he said the amount of money Mary earn could not pay the rent and feed both of you and you still have money to go gambling with so often.

Mary *starts screaming and groaning.*

Mary   I am no prostitute, what would my brother have to say about this.

Dickie   And to think that it's only this morning is the same vice squad man she was talking to on the street corner and in less than one hour, the same vice squad have her screaming the roof off the building.

Alvin   I will have to kill this woman.

Hazel   Oh God stop it, don't all of you think you have done enough for one day, hold on to your strength, Mary girl.

Byron   Don't you see the vice squad men carry two men off to jail this morning, not to mention Calvin who get nine months this morning.

Police sirens and dogs barking, **Alvin** *rushes to the window – everybody else freeze.*

Alvin   Bomboclath, the vice squad raiding the gambling house, come on let's go.

He gets skull cap and dark glasses from drawer.

Mary   Please don't go, Alvin, they will only take you to jail, please talk to him, Dickie.

Alvin   Shut your rassclath mouth. (*Slaps her to the ground.*)

Byron   Come on let's go.

Exit **Byron** *and* **Dickie** *and* **Alvin**. **Hazel** *puts her arms around* **Mary**.

Hazel   Take it easy, child. Lord God worries and troubles is going to kill Black people.

Mary   What am I going to do, Hazel? What's going to happen to me if Alvin goes to jail? I know the police don't like the type of person he is, I am sure he's going to fight with the police.

Hazel   Let's hope he don't. That Dickie have too much influence over him and Byron is such a bloody fool, you know something, they are right about one thing, the police have them fighting one another because the police know if they talk to us women on the street Black people think we are giving information to the police. Nobody don't need to inform on them because the police see them going in the gambling house so the police know they are drug smokers.

Mary   You are right, Hazel, you know, I really feel that the vice squad want the men to beat us up so we would inform on them. Why is Black people so stupid?

Hazel   Well, I don't think the police want to the Black men to beat us up but nobody don't know what a policeman is thinking except a policeman but the vice squad really make things difficult for us women because if you start telling Black people the truth about white people and the vice squad the Black people start calling you white man lover.

Mary   Does the vice squad do the same bad things to white people?

Hazel   Of course they do but in a different way, the Black people is too stupid to see the difference. The Black men are doing exactly what the vice squad want them to do.

Mary   But you did tell me that you did go out with a policeman once but I shouldn't tell anyone about it.

Hazel   Of course I did but that's all in the past now. He was the same policeman I used to go riding horses with up in Clifton but Dickie didn't know that he was a policeman, he thinks he knows everything, that's why he thinks that every white person who rides horses is rich.

Mary   Where did you meet him? Hazel, you have a lot of guts, I admire you for that.

Hazel   You have to have a lot of guts when you have a sick mother to keep in Jamaica which you have to send money to every month. With a load on your head and the hot blazing sun on your half-naked back the hunger in Jamaica is worse than the hunger in England and that same policeman I used to go riding with in Clifton he was quite a nice man. He was tall and handsome. He did take care of me for a while and then one day out of the blue he ask me to marry him, oh God I was so happy and pleased. He said that before he marries me I would have to move and live up in Clifton because most of the girls who live on St Paul's are prostitutes and the rest of them is rebel-rousing students, dirty beatniks and dirty drug-peddlers. Nice people don't live in St Paul's and I should live in Clifton where life is peaceful and quiet. I went home happily pack, and ready to move the next time I saw him was three months after standing at the corner of Grosvenor Road and Ashley Road in rasscloth uniform. I wasn't afraid of him I didn't care if every Black man in St Paul's see me talking to a policeman in uniform so I ask him why he never come back to see me he said his superior officer live up in Clifton and he see me and him riding horses together and every policeman down Bridewell Police Station know that I live in St Paul's because they see me talking to several white men on the street in St Paul's, God, I was so angry, shocked and depressed so I pull myself together and pluck up courage and start selling my pussy to several white men and I sell and sell and sell and keep my mother in Jamaica from starving and now I only said my pussy to one man. He's white, I loved him, he love me and I would marry him tomorrow if he ask me.

Mary   So all the evidence the vice squad need to call you a prostitute is to see you talking to a white man, Black people were born to suffer. We women can't win. If you live with a Black man he beats you up, if you talk to a white man you're a prostitute, or a informer. Lord God, we'd better leave before Alvin and the rest up and get back. I will have to go home with you to give Alvin time to cool off. I can't let my brother know about this.

Hazel   All right, and I'll come back with you later. No, I have got a better idea, let's go downstairs and hide in the toilet.

Exit **Mary** *and* **Hazel**.

Blackout

Light comes up to see **Alvin** *and* **Dickie** *walking the room talking.* **Byron** *making joint.*

Alvin   Look how the vice squad just grab up more Black people and take them down to jail. A where the rasscloth Mary is, I will kill her bloodclot today.

Bryon   Did you see when one of the Black man try to run out of the gambling house, the police dog set about him and nearly kill him. Man, did you notice how the dog and the policeman look like each other. Me sure white people are not human, a rasscloth, but why don't Black people organise, number us three to one, still if we were in America we would just shoot them down, to rassclot. Alvin you want to see the same vice squad man who was asking about you, he never stop looking at you, I think your dark glasses fool him. Man, he badly want to take you to jail. Still me glad they don't carry any of us to jail.

Dickie   Byron, shut your rasscloth. You think it's too late for the vice squad to come and take him to jail? Like you don't know what I am thinking. This maybe the next plays the vice squad raid. Man, don't you see what's happening? They raid two streets next to each other in one day. I would not be surprised if every single Black man in St Paul's end up in jail before the weekend. There is absolute nowhere else left for us to go at nights for a little recreation, except the blues dance on a Saturday night. You can't go to the club and enjoy yourself because it's always full with police and dogs ready to take you to jail. Look what happened last week in the club, one stupid white woman say Ranny thief her purse and the next thing you know is twenty policemen coming through the door with six police dog in front of them there is nowhere else left for us to go. Alvin, man, I think you'd better leave Bristol all together because you can't go up and live in Clifton, the vice squad will want to know what you are living in Clifton.

Alvin   The great British village bobby has never set foot in St Paul's. I can't run away, man, and what about Mary, I can't leave her. But where the rasscloth is she?

Byron   Maybe she pack her clothes and leave.

Alvin   She can't leave me, her clothes still in the wardrobe. She's only kidding because she knows I am going to kill her. But why the rasscloth vice squad want me alone, what do they want with me?

Byron How can they, when they want to lock you up? I suppose they want to take me to jail too. And I am ready to kill any one of them who come near me.

Alvin The loving great British village bobby never set foot in St Paul's.

Dickie Byron, make up the ganja.

He takes **Byron**'s *ganja and cigarette papers.*

Both start making joints.

Dickie Just let them vice squad walk through the bloodclot door today, boy, Black people have to come together to fight the pussy clot vice squad.

Alvin You know the best thing I think I better do is put a lot of make-up on my face the same way Dustin Hoffman did in the movie *Little Big Man*, so when I am walking about the street during the day the Vive Squad would think I am an old man and they wouldn't be able to recognise me.

Byron That's a good idea if you could become an old man, I am a carpenter, I could make you a couple of good walking sticks.

Dickie Man, the two of you is total fucking stupid, they might even think you are Dustin Hoffman, brother you may be able to hide from the vice squad because I know some of them still think every West Indian resembles Garfield Sobers. But let me tell you something, them rassclot vice squad police dogs know you so well that even if you hide in the bottom of the sea, the rass dogs would still recognise you, and start barking.

Byron Sometime I think those police dogs that they have searching for drugs see us so often that they know our names. They wouldn't just bark they would eat us.

Dickie Half the white people in this country have never seen a policeman. You are right, the British village bobby has never set foot in St Paul's, because those policemen that drive about in the Triumph and Rover they are not policemen; they are gentlemen who talk to motorists politely at traffic lights, but when the vice squad stop you on the street, the first question they ask you is if you want to fight, and if you the mistake and say yes, they will beat you there and then to death in the middle of the road, and man, you know what hurts me more than anything else is the way the English people use the word love all the fucking time. But it's long time I am in England, and white people can't for me. White people love is like a person who loves the night but cannot live without electric lights.

Byron A man that live all his life in St Paul's and die in old man and never meet a good white person because only the white vice squad people know us.

Alvin *panics, trying to get chairs and settee behind the door. He stops and puts the chairs, etc., back where they originally were.*

Alvin Byron, go and get your hammer and nails I am gonna nail up every door in the house. I am not going to sit here and let those rasscloth vice squad come here and carry me off to jail.

Dickie   Man, nailing up the door won't stop those rasscloth vice squad from breaking down the door with crowbar and sledgehammer.

Byron   But at least if the vice squad is going to smash the door down it would give Alvin a couple of minutes to get out through the window.

Dickie   Now what is the matter with you, you don't see how high the window is, you want the man to jump through the window and break his neck.

Byron   But he don't have to jump, he can always come down on a rope.

Dickies   Where is he going to get the rope? Boy, you are the worst fool in the world, you don't see that any time the vice squad raid any Black man's house, man and dogs around the house. Man, Alvin, you got no chance just to make up the ganja and smoke it, you might as well go to jail black up out of your mind.

Alvin *starts making a joint.*

Alvin   Man, if I was living with a white woman then maybe the vice squad would have a right to bother me, but is a Black woman I live with so no vice squad have any right at all to bother me. Man, the only chance I have got is two by two Alsatian dogs and let the dogs fight the vice squad.

Byron   I don't need nobody to tell me that I don't have any sense I know I am stupid, but no rascal of vice squad have any right at all to bother a matter whether he is living with a Black woman or a white woman Amanda to have a woman to do his rassclot vice squad have any rights at all to bother a man whether he is living with a Black woman or a white woman, a man need to have a woman to do his washing and cooking. So the rasscloth vice squad expect a man to live without a woman. Alvin, it would be very nice if you did buy the Alsatian dogs and feed the dogs on pure ganja tea so when the vice squad break your door down they come face to face with two mad Alsatian dogs. Boy, that would be the happiest day of my life.

Dickie   Boy, when I was younger I used to think that every white man was beautiful and the whole life was one big holiday with lots of friends, although they laugh and talk with each other, they don't like their one another. They just like to gang up against Black people, but I met a white man a long time ago who used to be manager of a big store and he told me that he used to laugh and talk with hundreds of people every day because he think it was his job to do so. So I ask him if all those people are his friends now, he tell me he doesn't have a single friend in the world, so half of these white people lived and died without the pleasure of having a friend. So since that day I stop becoming jealous of white men because I can't live with people who don't have friends. The only white person I have anything to do with is a white woman because when I first came to England the white woman were the only person who shows a little love and respect for the Black man. That's why I fool about with white chicks but I won't live with a white woman because every white woman work for the vice squad.

Dogs barking. Everybody freezes, panics and all rush to the window.

Alvin   Lord God, the vice squad is still over the gambling house. What the rasscloth are they still hanging around for? Dickey, quick, Byron, get down. They are taking photographs of the whole rasscloth street and two of the vice squad is looking over here. Please, God, don't let them find me.

They crawl on the floor back to where they were sitting.

Man, I have a feeling they are coming for me today. Where the rasscloth can I hide? Man, I need a shotgun. I bet they have photograph of me down the station. I am going mad.

He starts panicking, smoking joint and shaking.

I hope you realise that as soon as the vice squad come up here to arrest me Mary will have nowhere to live, the landlord is going to throw her out. What's going to happen to Mary if I go to jail, and it's not just the vice squad and the landlord, a man's got to worry about. Because as soon as you have to worry about the Black man they take you down to Bridewell Police Station this room will be full with Black men trying to share with your woman. I don't care what happens to me, but I am worried about Mary. Dickie, you and Byron will have to look after Mary if I go to jail.

Byron   Oh God, Alvin, of course we would, and don't worry about Mary, she's a good woman, she wouldn't look at another man. Man, Alvin, we are friends, we wouldn't let any man go near her. Listen, man, I have nowhere else to go, except to spend my whole life in St Paul's. You and Mary are the closest people to me in the whole world. Don't worry about Mary, she wouldn't let you down. Man, she really loves you.

Alvin   Boy, I only wish that sometimes Mary wouldn't bother me. I am not happy to see my woman working her fingers to the bone in a factory, the biggest rasscloth worries I have got is to make enough money and take Mary away from St Paul's and away from the rasscloth vice squad. Byron go and look out the window and see if the vice squad is still over the gambling house.

Byron *crawls to the window.*

Byron   Most of them is gone but three of them is still over there including the one with the ginger hair. One of them is standing at the door with a dog (*and he crawls back*).

Dickie   Bloodclot, the rest of them is only gone to get more police. Alvin, I tell you the vice squad will not stop until they have you and the rest of us in jail, but I am not going to no rasscloth white man prison, if they come over here, I am going to kill one of them and spend the rest of my life in prison. What's the difference St Paul's the biggest prison in England. Man, if you go down town and if anybody ask you where you live and you tell them you live in St Paul's they immediately think you are a thief, if you go to jail, Alvin, we're not sure if we can look after Mary because we will be the next to go to jail. Man, the vice squad will not stop until they have every Black man in jail. The thing that really hurts at the bottom of my heart is the big, rich white men, rich white men who live up in Clifton and leave their big houses and drive a big Jaguar car and come to St Paul's to buy pussy from the Black woman. All the Black woman have to do in St Paul's is to walk on the street and before five minutes ten white men will stop her, trying to buy her pussy. My woman cannot talk to a white man.

Alvin   Jesus Christ, the vice squad will have to leave me alone.

He starts panicking, smoking joint erratic.

I know I am going mad.

Enter **Mary** *and* **Hazel**.

Alvin   Where the rasscloth you been?

Pointing finger at **Mary**.

Alvin   I suppose you on the street talking to vice squad again. I hope you are happy now they are outside watching the house and ready to take me to jail, but I will make sure I kill you and one of them together before I go to jail.

Mary   I know one thing, you're not going to make me kill myself, have done nothing wrong or anything I am ashamed of. I am sorry I was talking to the vice squad this morning how was I to know that he was a policeman?

Alvin   How the rasscloth you should know? Didn't you know every white man is a policeman?

He starts talking towards **Mary**.

Alvin   A better bust your rasscloth head.

Hazel   Alvin, I know this is your house, and Mary is your woman, but you haven't done anything wrong. When I finish talking you can kill me if you like, I don't care. How you can believe that Mary have a nothing at all to do with the vice squad looking for you to arrest you and anyway, how do you know the vice squad is looking for you? Can't you see the police is making a fool out of the lot of you.

Dickie   Man, we will always hate some Black people. Since you know white people so well, and you seem to know exactly what the vice squad is thinking about us, so why don't you go outside and tell the vice squad to leave us alone. You are the one who is talking to them on the street corner when you are not fucking with other policeman. That's the reason why I sit down here and not say anything, minding my own business. Hazel, let me tell you something. You see all these white people have Black people and making them into traffic wardens it won't be long before every traffic warden in England is Black. I don't know what will happen to you by then because you are worse than a traffic warden.

Hazel   Dickie, why don't you go home and smell your woman's drawers, and leave me alone.

Dickie *moves quickly, slaps* **Hazel**. *She falls on the floor.*

Dickie   Don't fuck with me. I don't like woman who is cheeky. Don't let me have to throw your rasscloth through the window.

Heavy fast footsteps coming upstairs. Everybody panics. **Dickie** *dives under the bed and hides under the mattress.* **Byron** *and* **Alvin** *follow him.* **Mary** *makes the bed up.*

Hazel *helps her.* **Hazel** *and* **Mary** *sit on the bed.* **Hazel** *brushes her face and hair.* **Mary** *follows suit. Trying to act normally and look as if nothing has happened.*

Mary   Come in.

She goes to open the door. Comes back with card.

Lord God Almighty. Hazel, look. (*Hands card to* **Hazel**. *She looks at it.*)

Hazel   It's the telephone company come to connect your telephone. But I didn't know you were having a phone put in, Mary.

Mary   I don't know anything about telephone. It's Alvin. No wonder the vice squad was watching the house. And watching me, because what does Black people want with telephones in St Paul's.

Hazel   Well, I don't know two Black people in St Paul's who have telephones in their house.

Byron, **Dickie** *and* **Alvin** *'s heads appear from under the mattress.*

Mary   Take your rasscloth out of the house, Alvin. And don't come back bloodclot.

Hazel   As for you, Mr Dickie, I am going to kill you to bloodcloth. Who the rasscloth you think you slap?

She attacks **Dickie,** **Mary** *follows attacking* **Alvin.** **Byron** *in total panic. Gets away from the company and exits through door.*

Police siren, dogs barking. **Byron** *rushes back into room.*

Byron   Let's run to rass, man, they are coming again.

Byron, **Alvin** *and* **Dickie** *in total panic exit quickly.* **Mary** *and* **Hazel** *stand looking at each other in amazement.*

Blackout.

Shakespeare Country

Characters

Lucas
Norah
Herbie
Sally

First broadcast on BBC Two on 17 May 1973.
Director: Philip Saville
Producer: Tim Aspinall
Script Editor: Robert Buckler
Art Direction: Allan Anson

Cast
Alfred Fagon – Lucas
Carmen Munroe – Norah
Stefan Kalipha – Herbie
Merdel Jordine – Sally

Lucas *and* **Norah** *live in Fulham.* **Lucas** *is an actor, does very well as a Black actor, but has never made enough money to support his woman who is a nurse.*

Lucas*'s bedsitter. Day.*

Norah *is sitting in front of the mirror in pants and bra getting ready to go out.*

Lucas *is lying on the bed smoking a cigarette surrounded by books.*

Norah   Darling, I'm sure everything will be all right. Times have changed. Everybody knows that Othello is a Black man, even the other nurses at work are excited about you doing the part of Othello. You said yourself the director likes you. He wouldn't give the part to a white actor and I know you would make a great Othello. Don't worry, they will phone you today.

Lucas   Worried, I'm not worried.

Norah   Darling, I understand. Anyway it's my day off and I am determined that we will have a nice meal. Something special for my darling and myself. Would you like me to get you some cigarettes?

Lucas   I don't want anything.

He gets off the bed and looks at the telephone. **Norah** *looks at him.*

Norah   Oh, my sweet, sweet baby. I don't think I'll wear any tights today. It's a lovely day and I feel free and happy.

Lucas *looks at her passionately.* **Norah** *moves, hugs him.*

Norah   Darling, I won't be two ticks. I'll go straight to the bank and do my shopping as quickly as possible. God knows, I don't think I've got much left in the bank, so I'm sure there is enough to tide us over.

She kisses him.

Bye, darling, see you soon and please let me be your inspirator. By the way, are you going to see the probation officer this week?

Lucas   I don't know.

Norah   Okay. See you soon.

She exits.

Lucas   Why don't he call me? He promised he would call me today.

He puts the cigarette out. Lights another.

I know this will have to be my lucky break. I cannot take any more disappointment with a Shakespeare play.

He looks at telephone. Stamps his feet. The cigarette falls from between his fingers.

Oh hell!

He digs his heel in the carpet to put the cigarette out. Stands with his hands in his pockets.

Fourteen months was the last time I was on stage, and ever since, I've been hoping to get a television part like this.

Looks at the telephone, kicks chair.

Where am I going to get money from to pay bus fares? I'm tired of robbing the Underground. The Lord knows I cannot afford to get caught again, because they will surely send me to prison. I'm sure I am the best actor in England for that part. The director said he liked me. We even had a drink together.

He put his hands on his head, back against the door.

Goddam it, why don't those wicked people phone me? I'd better start smoking drugs like everybody else, but where the hell am I going to get the money from? They start filming in less than two weeks. I haven't even got the script yet.

Lights another cigarette.

God Almighty, I'm down to my last stick of matches and I haven't got a penny to buy another box.

Looks at telephone. Goes to the window.

I hope Norah brings some cigarettes back for me.

He goes to the cupboard, gets photos and press cuttings. Looks at them and smiles to himself. He reads one of the press cuttings.

I was good in that one. (*Looks at phone.*) They must call me today. I wonder what time it is?

Looks at watch, holds photo in front of him, goes over to the mirror.

I like this one.

Looks at himself in the mirror, looks at photo.

Jesus Christ, I'm getting old.

Looks at telephone, goes over to it and touches it.

My whole life depends on getting this job.

Telephone rings. He is completely frozen. One, two, three, four, he relaxes and picks the telephone up.

5523

Male Voice   Hello, Lucas. Well, about this part that I wanted you to play.

Lucas's *face changes as if he is going to collapse.*

Lucas   Hold it, Mr Assistant to Mr Assistant Assistant. To be or not to be? I haven't got the part.

Male Voice   No. But . . .

Lucas   Hold it, man of Shakespeare country.

Slams telephone down. He stands and stares at the wall for four to six seconds, shoots up hands above his head.

Yes, people of Shakespeare country, I have left you. Ever since I become an actor six years ago Shakespeare been domineering my life. I have never met you, Shakespeare. A mean the man been dead long before slavery started. What I've got to do is to make contact with my great-grandfather in Africa. I Lucas Grant hate you William Shakespeare.

He starts to jump up and down.

Yes, music.

Rushes over to record player, puts record on.

I am going to get you, Shakespeare.

Heavy African drums and singing – starts to dance a tribal war dance – taking his clothes off.

Lucas   Rumba, Humba, Kenyatta, Tshombi, Nboya, Nakruma. Allah, Allah give me strength so that I can destroy my enemies.

Takes all his clothes off down to his underpants – arms hanging low – looks like a gorilla – looks at wrist, sees watch, takes it off, smashing it through the window.

Music stops – starts moving furniture to the other side of the room – working very quickly – gets knife from the table, cuts carpet down the middle – throws half through the window – no furniture in half the room.

Rushes out of the room, comes back with two cans of paint, paintbrush. Red paint and white paint.

*Paints white line in the middle of the room, uses his fingers to put red and white paint on his face – groaning and slowly calming down – looking through window on empty side of room, back opposite the door – **Norah** enters.*

Norah   Jesus, what?

She puts the shopping bag down. Takes the cigarettes out.

Darling, what's wrong? Here I bought some cigarettes for you.

She moves across the white line to give him the cigarettes and to touch him. She touches him.

Darling!

Norah *sees the paint on his face for the first time.*

Lucas (*shouts in a broad American accent*)   Back off, woman. You come within range of me and you won't be around to do it again.

Norah *very shocked – backs away from him across white line.*

Norah   Oh, my God in heaven.

Lucas   From now on you better stay down wind of me. (*Stops speaking in an American accent.*) Didn't you see the white line? Never make the mistake to cross it again. The other side of the room belongs to you. This side belongs to me.

Norah   Here goes my knickers through the window. Gay Liberation Front here I come minus bra.

Lucas   You Shakespeare lover!

Norah   It happen again. You didn't get the television part. In case you forget, Shakespeare been dead for four hundred years or more. Damn you! Just look what you have done to the flat.

She gets very angry.

For the last year you have done nothing but smash the flat to pieces when you haven't got a part.

Lucas   Just look what I've got to put up with? A bloody nurse, not to mention that you are the most stupid nurse in the world, and to think that I spent all these years living with you. What good are you to me? You are a general in the British Army and a woman in glasses at the National Assistance Board. Yes, I'm finished with you but I am going to hell to find Shakespeare.

Norah   This time you have gone too far.

Lucas   Yes, as far as Shakespeare take me. Right now I feel good because I am getting closer to Shakespeare. Just stay away from me, that's all.

He starts looking around empty side of room for the knife which is lying somewhere on the floor.

Norah   Well, I am glad for you. Any minute now Shakespeare is going to walk into the room. I lost count of how many years I've been with you. Where is the great actor who was going to buy me a sports car and a flat in Chelsea? Surely, Lucas, you must realise how much I look after you. I don't mind spending my last two pounds on food – at least, please let us enjoy it together.

She moves forward. **Lucas** *springs forward knife pointing at* **Norah**. **Norah** *jumps back screaming.*

Norah   You bastard, you would, wouldn't you.

Lucas   Baby, you reading me loud and clear.

Norah   I've given up friends and everything that I ever work for. All the effort for a bloody madman.

Pointing at shopping bag.

That was the last two pounds I had in the bank. I don't get paid for another ten days. The labour exchange will not give you another penny. Yes, this time you've gone too far.

Lucas *points the knife at her.*

Lucas   Next time do your investing in the building society.

Norah   I knew those books would drive you crazy and now you want to cut my throat with the knife.

Lucas   Anyway, why should I? When I could lay you out with one punch.

Looks at knife.

This is going to help me get closer to Shakespeare, and you will be left alone to face the people of Shakespeare country. Yes, you have spent the last two pounds and I got to move onto better things. No more last two pounds for me. Yes, the time has come.

Sticks knife in one of the Xs in wall. Grabs paintbrush, writes 'Shakespeare' between the two Xs.

There is writing on the wall. Go thy way, woman, and tend thy sick.

Norah   Oh no, Lucas Grant, all of them put together is not as sick as you. Yes you really sick.

Lucas   Me sick!

Pointing at writing on the wall.

My grandfather used to cook and eat people like him. (*Grabs knife.*) Fourteen months Shakespeare was the last time the curtain rose for me.

Norah   Lucas, please what are you talking about?

She starts walking towards **Lucas**.

Norah   Lucas, darling, please give me the knife.

Lucas *moves forward pointing the knife at* **Norah**. **Lucas** *is very aggressive, eyes blazing.*

Lucas   Stay away from the white line or I will change my mind and take you with me to find Shakespeare.

Norah (*backs away from him*)   He is right next to you on the wall. I'm going to phone the probation officer.

Lucas   While you are at it, phone God and tell him I'm going to hell to find Shakespeare.

Norah *very sad and worried, still clutching packet of cigarettes.*

Norah   Please don't completely destroy yourself.

Lucas *starts humming song.*

Norah   Have a cigarette. You'll feel better. Please, Lucas.

Norah *moves towards him.*

Lucas (*shouting*)   Back off, woman! (*Screaming.*) Have a cigarette. Keep your poison for your Shakespeare friends. I was hot as hell on the banana boat coming over here and it was hot as hell in Jamaica but it is nowhere as hot as my insides in this cold Shakespeare country.

He starts running around in circles.

The wind, the wind.

Norah (*shouting*)   Was it the wind that caused you to throw bricks through the theatre window because they were doing *Hamlet*? Shakespeare is right behind you on the wall. Why you don't you put the wind up him?

Lucas   I need no aeroplane ticket to get away from Shakespeare country.

Norah (*puts a cigarette in her mouth*)   Lucas, look. I'm going to start smoking again. You said that smoking was bad for me. Come on, Lucas, tell me to put the cigarette down.

Lucas   The north wind, the south wind, the east wind and the west wind. The first one that comes along will take the spirit away to find Shakespeare. I've got to make myself very strong.

Puts knife in between his teeth. Starts to do press-ups. General exercise. **Norah** *rushes from the room. Returns with a bucket of water. Throws water over* **Lucas**.

Norah   The body must be cleansed before the spirit leaves. When you first started acting it was the Smiths, the Jones and the Browns who were stopping your soul from finding peace, but over the last few years all I hear from you is that if you are not a Shakespearean actor nobody will employ you and that's a damn lie! Shakespeare is dead – dead. Do you hear me?

Lucas *is still humming.* **Norah** *gets the London Underground poster – pointing at poster.*

Norah   This is what you've got to worry about. Fifty pounds fine, first offence, second time a hundred pound fine or three months imprisonment. You've got caught six times. The probation officer is getting tired of you. This is your biggest problem. Not bloody Shakespeare.

Throws poster at him.

Why don't you put your clothes on and go on the street and fight the Smiths, Jones and Browns?

Lucas   It's the north wind. (*Screaming.*) Shakespeare, I want to see your face. Aaaahhhh!

Norah *grabs the bucket, starts hitting him with it. The bucket falls to the ground,* **Norah** *rushes over and starts fighting to get the knife away from him.*

Norah   No. Lucas, no. (*Hysterical.*) Please, Lucas. Somebody help me. Somebody please help me.

Sudden knocking at door. Door opens and **Sally** *and* **Herbie** *enter.* **Herbie** *grabs* **Lucas** *and* **Sally** *grabs* **Norah**. *They back away.* **Norah**'*s hand is bleeding.*

Herbie   Hold it, man! What's happening? Control yourself, man.

Sally   She's bleeding.

Norah   He's going to kill himself.

Herbie   Sally, get the first-aid kit.

Sally (*hugging* **Norah**)   It's all right, come on, it's all right.

Sally *rushes from the room.*

Herbie   What's this, Lucas, man?

Lucas (*calmly*)   Man, I'm tired.

Norah   Why, Lucas? Why?

Herbie *lets go of* **Lucas**. **Lucas** *walks across the room and sits in a chair* – **Norah** *kneels beside him.* **Herbie** *is looking around the room.*

Norah   You don't have to be an actor if you don't want to.

Hugging **Lucas**'*s leg.*

Norah   We will manage.

Herbie *looks at the writing on the wall.*

Herbie   Wow!

Norah   I love you.

Sally *enters with the first-aid kit and water – she starts to wash* **Norah**'*s hand.*

Norah   I am sorry, Sally.

Sally   Whatever for. This is what friends are for.

She looks at the cut,

Oh, it's not too bad. You want to go to the hospital?

Norah   No it's alright. Just bandage it for me.

Herbie (*still cannot believe his eyes*)   What happen, Norah?

Norah   I don't know.

Sally   What's that on Lucas's face, and the room!

Norah   Thanks, Sally. Lucas, I'll get some hot water for your face.

Sally   It's alright I'll get it.

Herbie   Wow! What happen, Lucas man?

Sally   Shut up, Herbie. Can't you see he is in a state of shock. I'll get the water.

Lucas   No it's okay I am going to the bathroom.

He exits.

Herbie   What happened, Norah?

Sally   Can't you wait?

Norah   I don't know. I just don't know.

Sounds of **Lucas** *washing his face.*

Norah   I went shopping this morning. Lucas was waiting for a telephone call about a television part. When I came back the room was like this. And he in talking about Shakespeare, and that he was going to travel on the wind. I don't understand it.

Herbie   Well, did he get the television part?

Norah   No, I don't think so.

Sally   Is that why he went crazy?

Norah   You see, sometimes I don't know if he's acting or if he's serious, but he blew his mind this morning.

Herbie   I just don't know what's wrong with Lucas. He never leaves his damn books alone these days.

Sally   Never mind about his books look what he's doing to Norah. Every time he doesn't get a part he takes it out on her.

Norah   What am I going to do, Sally?

Sally   Well, anytime he do anything like this again, get rid of him. What kind of maniac is he?

Norah   He spends all his time reading Shakespeare plays these days.

Herbie   Wait a minute. The part that he didn't get this morning – is it the Black Othello they are doing for television?

Norah   Yes.

Herbie   I know they wouldn't give it to a Black man.

Norah   I will have to straighten the room out.

Sally   No, it's all right. Me and Herbie will do it.

She starts clearing the room up.

Herbie   Look how long me and the man been friends? Why doesn't he stop trying to be the greatest Shakespeare actor? I beg him to come with me on my last interview – I'm sure he would have got a part in the film. Why does he spend all his time worrying about Shakespeare?

Norah   Herbie, I'm only a nurse. You are an actor and his friend. You should know.

Sally   Will you stop worrying about Lucas and his hang-ups? Why don't you ask him yourself about Shakespeare?

Herbie   I will. Look how happy he was when we were going to drama school. He was the best Shakespeare actor in his class. Everybody thought he was going to be so successful.

Sally   Well, he's not successful now. Will you please help me move the furniture?

Norah   Oh, Sally, I feel so helpless, I should be helping you.

Herbie   It's all right, Norah, I'll do it in a minute. I used to sit and listen to Lucas for hours about how important it was for Black actors to get involved in Shakespeare's plays. All the teachers at drama school convinced him that he would make a great Othello. We all believed the teachers because he was a good Shakespeare actor, especially Othello.

Sally   Now will you help me?

Herbie   Okay, okay, I will. What a sad way to see Lucas.

Starts helping **Sally** *with the furniture.*

Enter **Lucas***.*

Norah   Your socks are in the bottom drawer.

Lucas   Thank you.

Herbie   How you feeling, man?

Lucas   I'm okay. How are things with you?

Herbie   Wow, man, great. Listen to this. I got the part.

Sally (*very excited*)   I was coming down to tell you, Norah. I am so happy for Herbie.

Norah   I'm glad for both of you.

Lucas   What's the story about?

Sally   It's a James Bond type.

Herbie   Yeah, man, it's about a very rich English couple. Well, you see, they had a son who deserted the British Army, and is giving information to the East Germans – so this rich couple decided to go to East Germany and kidnap their son. You know, take him back to England. Man, I'm really happy. Yeah, man, really happy.

Lucas   What's your part like?

Herbie   Oh yeah, man, I am their chauffeur. I am in it from start to finish. Goddamn it, man, one hundred and thirty-five pounds per week.

Norah   That's very good.

Sally   I am so happy.

Lucas   I suppose they will give you a uniform. Another Black and white minstrel production, except they didn't have to use boot polish on you.

Sally (*grabs* **Herbie***'s hand*)   Oh, he's so beautiful I love him.

Herbie   Man, things are happening for Black actors these days.

Lucas   Yes, man, I read about it every day, and I agree with you but nothing is happening for the nigger actor. Not everybody who is Black is a nigger.

Norah (*moves across to* **Lucas**)   You all right, darling?

Lucas   Stop darling, darling me.

Sally   I think we'd better leave, Herbie.

Norah   What? You only just got here.

Herbie   What's eating you, man?

Salky   Yes, what's bothering you, Lucas? What the hell are you hinting at? You smash your own flat up. What do you want from us? Go back reading your damn books.

Herbie   Sally, baby, please.

Sally   Shut up to hell. What's wrong with you? Can't you see what he's trying to do to you? Imagine your best friend, and you just had a film part for one hundred and thirty-five pounds per week and he don't even congratulate you. Let's go back to our flat.

Herbie   Take it easy, baby. Listen, man, we grew up together in Jamaica. We were friends and we still are friends now, and don't forget you are the one who encouraged me, and how we were going to be famous and become the greatest Black actors that ever lived.

Lucas   Yes, that's true. But I'll tell you something that I didn't know then. That this is Shakespeare country for Shakespeare people.

Sally   What the hell Shakespeare got to do with anything. Can't you see he's gone crazy?

Herbie   Take it easy baby. Man, I'm not sure what's eating you. Why are you talking me like this? I'm not a token nigger and I think that's what you think I am in this movie. Man, they are paying me one hundred and thirty-five pounds per week.

Lucas   Herbie, when we were at school, how much money did we use to have for our lunch?

Herbie   Penny-a-penny.

Sally   Isn't that fantastic? And now he's getting one hundred and thirty-five pounds per week.

Norah   Excuse me. (*She exits.*)

Herbie   Get to the damn point, man. This is a very big break for me. I don't know of any Black actor in England or America who did lead parts in any production before they do a lot of extra work. Sidney Poitier, Harry Belafonte and guys like that who made it, they are all from poor families. So forget about having penny-a-penny to buy a-penny sugar, and penny worth of bread for lunch in Jamaica, and that's exactly what we used to have. This is England, 1972, not Jamaica, 1950.

Sally   That's right, you tell him.

Lucas   Herbie, I went crazy in this room today. For the first time in my life. I was positive beyond all doubt that Shakespeare was the manager for every producer and director, in this very big and powerful acting country.

Sally   Why? Because you didn't get the television part?

Lucas   Man, every nigger who made it to the top is from a poor and pitiful background, because if he's from what these people of Shakespeare country call a good home he'd be a white man with a Black skin. You see, my friend, anyone who sits in the sun long enough will eventually get a Black skin, but to be born a nigger is something else.

Sally   You're only jealous. They didn't want you for the television part and Herbie got the film part.

Herbie   Shut up, Sally, cool it. Man, there is no colour bar in the theatre. Man, they are the greatest group of people I've ever met.

Lucas   We don't seem to understand each other since we have become actors. I am not talking about colour bar. I am also not talking about the skin of a man. I'm talking about this bloody bastard soul. That is what acting is all about.

Norah *enters with tray full of cups and saucers, etc. for coffee but no coffee pot.*

Sally   Norah, your hand! Please let me help you.

Norah   It's all right, I can manage.

Sally   Damn you, Lucas. Take your bloody soul to hell. You're no damn good. I know that everything that's in this flat Norah pays for it.

Herbie   Cool it, baby.

Sally   Cool it, baby, your arse.

Norah   Sally, please.

Sally   It's damn embarrassing. He smash your flat to pieces and I suppose he expects you to still feed him.

Lucas   You are nothing, Sally, just a stupid backside and two large tits. Three years I spent in drama school, done nothing over the last two years except read Shakespeare plays. (*Looking at books.*) Years I spent reading about Greek theatre.

He throws books one at a time onto the floor.

All the way through to the Romans. I read philosophers from Socrates to Bertrand Russell.

He moves across to the bed where all of Shakespeare's plays are lying including a large Oxford dictionary.

I know Shakespeare's plays inside out.

He picks up the dictionary and Othello.

Norah (*stands*)   Darling, please.

Lucas *looks at her very hard.*

Norah   I'm sorry.

She moves and sits down.

Sally   What's the matter with you, Norah? Why are you so afraid of him?

Herbie   Jesus Christ.

Lucas (*looking at* Othello)   The months and weeks I spent on this one. I checked every word in it with the Great Oxford Dictionary.

Throws the dictionary away. It falls near to **Sally***'s feet.*

Sally   Just watch where you are throwing your stupid books.

Lucas (*looking at* Othello)   This one is a Black man.

Sally   Yes, baby, a Black man. (*Starts laughing.*) Oh God, you really are funny.

Lucas *and* **Herbie** *look very hard at* **Sally***.* **Norah** *moves across to the window and looks out.*

Sally   What's the matter?

Looking at **Herbie***. She sits back shaking her legs.*

Lucas   Herbie, this is the biggest crime ever committed against any nigger actor. (*Pointing at* Othello.) I hate your Black bastard face. This is a white English man with black paint on his face. Any white man can put boot polish on his face and become another Black bastard to a white man. Shakespeare's play is for Shakespeare's English people. (**Lucas** *grabs* **Herbie**.) Tell me, friend, can a nigger put white paint on his face and become a white man? Get out, you punk.

Herbie   What?

Norah   Lucas, darling.

Lucas   I told you before, don't darling me. You heard me, man, take your arse out of here.

Starts pushing **Herbie***.*

Norah (*grabs* **Lucas**)   That's your best friend.

Lucas *pushes* **Norah** *away. He opens door and pushes* **Herbie** *out.*

Lucas   And wait for your bastard stupid whore. (**Lucas** *grabs* **Sally**.) Get out, you stupid bitch.

Sally   Take your bastard hands off me.

Lucas   Get out. (*Kicks her through the door.*)

Norah   Shall I go too?

Lucas   It's your flat, baby, you're the one who's paying the rent. Remember, fifteen months no work.

Norah   I want to look you straight in the eye. (**Norah** *walks across room, stands looking at* **Lucas** *who is sitting down.* **Norah** *slaps his face.*) Pig, dirty pig. What do you think you are, a kept stallion? Oh, God, I hate you. Why, Lucas, you sit here destroying yourself and everybody that loves you? Remember when you were fifteen you ran away from home to become a seaman. Five years I waited for you. Look at me when I am talking to, you bastard. You told me then that you wanted to become an actor.

(*She picks up Socrates.*) This was the man you talked about all the time. You said the he opened your eyes to so many different things, and the only way you could express yourself was to become an actor. Next time we met was in church. We waited until everyone left the church. I gave you this. (*She puts the book at his feet – goes to cupboard.*) You gave me this Bible. Look at it, Lucas, we made love there and then in God's good church with the Bible in my hand. Oh, God how we loved each other. Let us go to England you said. I am going to take the world by its throat and shake it. Those were your exact words. One week after that we were on the banana boat destination England, not Shakespeare country. This is England, you will have to change if you want to live here. England is our home and it is full of English people. It is too late to go back to childhood dreams. We have nowhere else to go so you will have to change and learn to live with English people.

Lucas   I should change. Who are the criminals for hundreds of years, Shakespeare and his English gangsters. Bloody sex gangsters – I should change? And start masticating myself, because of lesbians and queers? My grandfather and myself have committed no crime against Shakespeare and his sex maniacs. How can a nigger change to a white man and keep his soul? You know what I did the last time I worked? I had to kiss a man. How does it feel when you see me kissing a man? Now you look me in the eyes. This is Shakespeare country for Shakespeare sex maniacs.

He goes to cupboard. Takes out a bag and start packing some clothes.

Norah   I can look you in the eye. You don't know nothing. I love every part of your body. Long before you were seven years of age. I have got two arms, two legs and a pair of eyes. There is no mistake about my sex. I am your woman since I was four years of age. I carry the same love for you to this very second. I work with you in the fields planting potatoes when I was twelve in the blazing hot sun with our naked backs. (*She rushes over and starts hitting* **Lucas**.) You bastard. You cruel, dirty bastard. (*She stops hitting him. She screams.*) I am your woman. (*She starts crying.*) I plant the same potatoes with you in your Shakespeare country. Just think, Lucas. Look at the way we live. We have never think about getting married, because there was never any doubt in our minds that we were going to spend the rest of our lives together. Acting completely runs your life now and take away your mind and soul. But I am still a person and you have taken off into thin air. If only you could take your body where you put your mind. Right now I am looking at the man I grew up with and tell me who are you? Yes, Lucas I know, after all these years it comes to an end. Please you must tell me which road to take. (*She screams.*) You cheated me. When you find your grandfather. You don't want a woman on your conscience. Yes, Lucas, I am a white woman to you. That is what coming to England done for me. (*She slaps his face.*) Look at my body, you bastard, I am human.

Lucas   How can I be human in a country like this? The kind of love that you're talking about doesn't exist in England. There no river for us in Shakespeare country, to have a bath before we go to church on Sunday. This place would turn God into a queer. All I know is that I am an actor and when I go for interviews the man look at me and I don't look like one of his Shakespeare disciples. So I sit there looking at him and watch his face turn into confusion. You see, he don't even have time to think about you as a person because his mind is always in the middle of a sex war. All of Shakespeare people see you as a sex maniac. (*He grabs her.*) I am a Black nigger actor in England, and for fourteen years all I hear about is Sidney Poitier and Harry Belafonte. Imagine, you have to tell grown people on TV to *Love They Neighbour* and we will show you how to live like a white man. The Jamaica we left not there anymore. It came to Shakespeare country with us when we left, but Shakespeare people make sure that we couldn't keep it. All they know to do is to laugh at niggers and the same niggers they are laughing at like to pay ten pounds to go to Australia. Niggers are not allowed, that's Shakespeare people sense of humour for you. I finish with you? I would finish with Jesus Christ and the Virgin Mary if they were living in Shakespeare country like white people. (*He continues packing.*)

Norah   It's not like that for Black actors in America. We could go there.

Lucas   England is where I spent fourteen years of my life not in bloody America, and every newspaper I pick up I read in it that niggers and white people don't use the same toilets in South Africa.

Norah   Where will you go, Lucas? Oh, I forget your great-grandfather's.

Lucas   Everywhere you go in London there are nigger embassies all over the place, and all they are doing is to give parties for people like Herbie. Since the day I came to Shakespeare country, those niggers in the embassies have never done anything for niggers like myself. I hope Shakespeare people shoot the bastard lot of them. They and their bastard parties dancing to Regge Regge Here Comes Johnny Regge. You want go and live with somebody like Herbie, so he could take you to the parties they have in the nigger embassies. Herbie must have saved my life a hundred times, and just look at him now. Yeah, man, one hundred and thirty-five pounds per week! All he talks about is the white sandy beaches of Jamaica. He never see any white beaches. The only thing we used to see when we were there was a shotgun pointing up our backside. 'Drop it, what are you doing on my land?' I came to Shakespeare country, fourteen years travelling on the London Underground reading advertisements for ten pounds you could do it in Australia and stamp across your soul . . . niggers rejected. You come home, open a can of fruit and eat it then right in front of your eyes and empty can in front of you, you read packed in Australia, and a stupid kangaroo laughing at you. You feel sick and run to the toilet because you know I have just eaten your grandfather's blood. I want to free my soul of sex maniacs and super niggers. (*He closes bag and goes to leave.*)

Norah   Your grandfather of Africa and your soul in eternity. For thirty years I have been your lover, mother and grandfather. When the teddy boys nearly beat you to death it was me – Norah – the white woman who nursed you and put the blood back in your veins. I did not have a penny in the house, so it was a Nora the White Woman who went out and stole soup in the supermarket to feed you. (*She screams.*) You didn't know I was a thief did you? Yes, I read plenty of books too, Lucas, on how to care for your body. That's the only reason why I became a nurse. So that if my man Lucas ever become ill again I would know how to care for him. Every time you bleed I bleed with red blood running out of my veins like yours. Damn you! When you were dying I read books on how to care for you. I walked through the same mud holes, sat in the same school room and picked the chigger from your feet and the lice from your hair and I've done more than that for you in your Shakespeare country.

Lucas   The wind that blows over my grandfather's dead body . . . I, Lucas Grant, feel it in my lungs in every breath I take.

He takes suitcase and goes.

Norah (*running after him*)   I am coming with you.

Lucas *stops, turns and looks at her. He comes back into room and sits down. He smiles at her. Pause.*

Lucas   Alright, get your things together.

Norah *gets out a small case and starts to pack.* **Lucas** *goes to photos and press cuttings and rips them up.*

Norah   I am ready.

They leave together.

End.

Small World

Characters

John, *thirty-three to thirty-five, Black, born in Kilburn, medium size*
Beatrice, *fifty-nine to sixty, Jamaican, plumpish*
Buster, *sixty-two to sixty-four, Jamaican, stockily built*
Elaine, *late twenties, Black Londoner, slim*
Jane, *twenty-four to twenty-five, white, English, slim*
Brendan, *late twenties, white Irish, slim*
Rama, *sixty to sixty-two, West Indian, chubby*
Shirley, *thirty-seven to thirty-nine, West Indian, just above medium*
Terrence, *twelve to fourteen, Black, slim*
Leonard, *early twenties, Black Londoner, slim*
Charkey, *early twenties, Black Londoner, slim*
Denzil, *early twenties, Black Londoner, slim*

Act One

Scene One

Lights.

Buster *and* **Beatrice** '*s front room. Friday between midnight and 4 a.m.*

John *standing with case in front of him, lights cigarette.*

Beatrice (*from halfway down staircase*)   Is that you, John?

John   Yes, Mother.

Beatrice   Put away the crowbar, Buster, it's John.

Beatrice *enters front room.*

Beatrice   Ah, son, how are you. (*She hugs him.*) Why don't you sit down. Oh it's warm tonight. Cup of tea.

John   No thanks, Mother.

Buster   Boy, you look bust-up. Wake up, man.

Beatrice   He is tired.

Buster   Overwork as usual. Sit down, son, shake up yourself or go to bed.

Beatrice   You have got a suitcase with you.

John   Yes I would like to stay for a few days.

Buster   What's the matter, you hit her?

Beatrice   Shut up, Buster, my boy would never do that. Not that he couldn't, but he wouldn't.

John   Thanks, Mother. Ah well, such is the way of life.

Beatrice   Strong, my boy is strong. Look at him, he works day and night for the citizens of this neighbourhood.

Buster   Yes, but he is weak in some ways.

Beatrice   What, you must be joking. What about a little food, son. Chicken and rice and peas is waiting for you and a little stewed beef as well.

Buster   Have you started drinking again? I mean I have a bottle of brandy handy.

John   No, no it's alright, had an argument with her that seems to last for days. I couldn't take it anymore.

Buster   Yes, man, I thought so. Did you hit her?

Beatrice   Oh, Buster you're so barbaric, why should he hit his wife?

Buster   Well, suppose she is two-timing him?

Beatrice   Modern days young couple do not hit each other.

Buster   Who said so?

Beatrice   My boy would never lay a finger on any woman.

John   No, no, no it's not like that. But we do fight, but not with our hands.

Buster   What do you use bottles?

He sits.

Beatrice   Not every man is like you.

Buster   I know because you're the first one who always hit me.

Beatrice   You're a born troublemaker, you same Buster. What about some food, son, you still haven't sit down.

John   No I don't want any food. I would just like to talk to the both of you.

Beatrice   Yes, of course, son. Have you talked to your brother recently?

She sits in easy chair.

John   Yes he phoned me the other day, said he's putting his house up for sale and then he's going to Canada.

Beatrice   Hope he comes to see us before he goes away.

John   Of course he will.

Beatrice   But he haven't phoned or come to visit us for such a long time.

Buster   He's only hot-headed, that's all.

Beatrice   Yes, I suppose so.

John   He always help with the football team whenever he can.

Buster   Do you think you will win the cup this year?

John   Dad, I don't know how much longer I can keep the advice centre going. I mean I don't want to give up.

He sits down

Beatrice   You're not going to throw away so many years of hard work are you?

John   I can't help it. While I'm trying to solve other people's problems, my own life is falling apart with great seas of difficulties in front of me.

Beatrice   So young to be so sad. You must find happiness whatever the price. I mean play your cards right, it will work out. So how is she?

John   Seems to be twice as happy as me.

Buster   Man, so how is the football team, those young guys look very brave to me.

John   It's alright for them, that is all they live for.

Beatrice   What do you mean, son? They're only following your advice.

John   I know, but what kind of future are they going to have?

Buster   It is wrong for you to get so emotionally involved with your work. Man, train the football team to win the cup. Is it still an all-Black team?

John   No.

Buster   I haven't seen them play for a while.

Beatrice   Why don't you have a drink with your father.

John   Okay, I'll have some orange juice.

Buster   Right then. I will put your case upstairs since I'm going to get the brandy.

He exits with case.

Beatrice   Come in the kitchen with me. Make yourself at home. It was nice of you to come and see us.

Buster (*from top of stairs singing*)
Me want go, me can't go, Japanese a go sink the ship.
Me want to go, we can't go Japanese a go the ship.
Brown-skin girl stayed home and mind baby, for I am going away on a sailing ship and if I don't come back, stay home and mind baby.

Starts humming.

John   Why does he always sing those songs?

Beatrice   Only when he drinks, and anyway they are songs from the war days.

John   Why remember rubbish things like war?

Beatrice   War was the reason why he came here in the first place. And after the war he invite me to join him in Kilburn, London. We grew up together so we love each other from baby days.

John   I know.

Beatrice   Let's give thanks to God you don't have to fight in any war. I will go and get your orange juice.

She exits.

John   Thanks. (*Talking to himself.*) This wife of mine is smashing my life to pieces. Did I make a mistake? Who is to blame? Who is wrong? My God, what's wrong with me? I am normal like anyone else, except that I'm trying to help Black people.

Buster *enters.*

Buster   Hold your horses, son. If you're going to talk to yourself don't talk so loud. All right, what happened?

Brandy in hand, he gets two glasses.

John   I need to sort out my life.

Buster   Yes, man, because you're so busy all the time doing other things other than doing what you are supposed to be doing with your wife.

John   That's not my fault.

Buster   You taking a shot?

He gives him brandy and glass.

John   No, mother is getting me some orange juice.

Buster   I'll lay you a fiver she'll bring your plate of food as well.

John   I don't gamble

Buster   I do.

John   That's your problem.

Buster   So tell me, why you leave your wife?

John   I haven't left her, I just need a break that's all.

Buster   Marriage on the rocks, eh?

John   It seems to be heading that way.

Buster   Anyone else involved?

John   No, I don't think so.

Buster   But you have your doubts?

John   It's not easy living with her and running the advice centre.

Buster   You still love her?

John   Yes, but love only seems to go skin deep these days.

Buster   It was like that all the time, except people use to depend on each other. These days, it's not like the war days when we all used to muck in with each other. In those days I used to have some friends me like your mother and me, school days sweetheart. Well, John, you know the house is yours, so you can talk when you feel like it. It is quite a few years now since you get married and this is the first time you pack a suitcase and leave your wife. Your mother will be very worried about this situation that you find yourself in at this most unfortunate hour of the night.

Beatrice *enters carrying tray with stewed steak, chicken, rice and peas, carrot juice, glass of milk, knife and fork.* **John** *looks at her in amazement.* **Beatrice** *is standing in front of* **John**. **Buster** *bursts out laughing,* **John** *joins in laughter.* **Beatrice** *smiles broadly.*

Beatrice   You must eat. And drink some milk for strength.

John   Well, I am hungry, but I did not realise I was.

Beatrice   That's a good boy.

John *takes tray from her, puts tray on coffee table. Picks up sausage with fork.*

John   I see you still eating pork.

Beatrice *sits in easy chair.*

Buster   Man, stop your foolishness. The first piece of meat to eat in this house is pork. Boy, leave the sausage for me, I will eat it. Pork is the sweetest meat I ever tasted.

John   All right. Well thanks, Mother. (*He eats as if he hasn't had a meal all week.* **Beatrice** *and* **Buster** *sit watching him.*) Jesus Christ, for days I forget to eat. Elaine haven't cooked all week and I didn't have time to cook for myself. Once upon a time Elaine was a good wife. Now she thinks I'm stupid running the advice centre. It's nearly three years now since I opened the advice centre and a lot of youths from my centre are now married and have a steady job. A few went to jail. I am sorry about the few that are still in jail. But what else can I do except in continuing to try and keep the rest of them out of prison. Mother, your hand is still very sweet. I don't think I can manage the milk, but the carrot juice is really nice.

Beatrice   That's alright, son. The carrot juice have plenty of milk in it. Give the milk to me, I will drink it.

John *gives milk to* **Beatrice**.

Beatrice   Thanks, son, nice to see you have such a healthy appetite. (**John** *continues eating.*) So where is Elaine now? (**John** *continues eating.*)

John   At home, moaning. She doesn't want to teach at the centre anymore. She said next Saturday morning will be her last lesson.

Beatrice   But why?

John   She said she can't teach Black history to kids who is only interested in football. Yeh, Dad, that we have a new coach, a young Irishman, he's got a touch of Georgie Best in him.

Buster   Yes, but does he drink as much?

John   He doesn't drink alcohol.

Buster   What, I've never met an Irishman who doesn't drink.

John   Then you haven't met many Irishmen.

Buster   Boy, stop your foolishness. It's forty-one year I live in Kilburn. Any day that the Englishman declare war on the Irishman this is the first place the Air Force would bomb.

John   You talk about the Irish as if they were Russians.

Buster   Not me, I drink with them every day. I have never had a drink with any Russian.

John   You are like the rest of them, you see the Irish as if they are drunks like every Russian is a soldier. Jesus Christ, people talk about the Russian and the Irish as if no woman has ever set foot in those countr. Even the dirty jokes them about the two country is about men, not like the jokes them about England where the number one joke is about the vicar's daughter. And now these rich and famous MP is fighting over Page 3 girl in the House of Parliament. How could Winston Churchill beat Hitler with sex maniacs like these?

Buster   Boy, stop your foolishness. Beatrice had better go to bed, your son is mad.

Beatrice   Buster, you are too dramatic.

Buster   But how can you do this to me? When I was in the Jamaican battalion of foot soldiers who were the first to set foot in Berlin when we were helping Mr Churchill to lick Hitler's arse.

John   Jesse James did more than all of you put together.

Buster   What was he, a Coca-Cola general in the American army?

John   No, he was a runner.

Buster   That's right, because the Americans didn't come into the war until the end. Yes that's right, they're all runners not like us who stand fast to our tommy guns.

John   Are you blind? You don't see the American is taking on the rest of the world and beating them all into the ground.

Buster   Boy, the English army is the best trained in the world.

John   Listen, I don't want to talk about stupid soldiers. I came here for a bit of peace and quiet.

Beatrice   Yes, that's right, son. Let's talk about Elaine.

John   No, I want to talk about myself. I'm the one with all the problems.

Buster   Elaine is right.

John   What is she right about?

Beatrice   Buster, don't upset him.

John   You don't care much for the advice centre do you? Except for the football team. Why aren't you rejoicing over the West Indian cricket team that is hammering England all over the Caribbean.

Buster   Didn't have time to play cricket when I was younger.

John   Well, I thought everybody who was born in the West Indies was a cricket fan.

Buster   Yes, like every Irishman born in Ireland is a drunk. Boy, it seems like you are going to make twice as many mistakes as myself.

Beatrice   At last you're admitting the truth that you make lots of mistakes.

John   My marriage is not over. Elaine just needs to see a bit of sense, that's all. The only mistake that I can possibly make its to give up the advice centre.

Buster   That would be a blessing, not a mistake.

John   Are you serious?

Buster   Yes let's be serious.

John   Okay. What do you propose I do?

Beatrice   All right, this is where I think I will go to bed, but remember, we have neighbours so please confine your shouting match within these four walls. John, I am deeply sorry about the relationship you were having with your wife. Try and make it up to her, she always seems the perfect wife for you.

John   That is because you don't have to live with her twenty-four hours a day.

Buster   John there is no Martin Luther King in England if you want a slice of bread you will have to go out and work for it when you get older the only friend you're going to have is a fat bank account look at you a nervous wreck if it wasn't for that advice centre you have no problem with your wife.

John   The day that I give up my advice centre is the day that every Black man is liberated in England and everywhere else in the world yes look at you fighting the last war and what did you get out of it you are my father what's in it for me.

Buster   Boy, I have my wife and a bottle of brandy in front of me, my house and two grown-up sons.

John   Do you expect me to do nothing for the poor Blacks of Kilburn?

Buster   No, but at least get rich first and make it easy on yourself.

John   I am not starving.

Buster   I know, you're in the middle of eating a large plate of food.

John   All right, why aren't you rich?

Buster   If I was your age with your education I would be.

John   You was once my age.

Buster   I had to fight in the war.

John   Okay, Dad, I really don't know if you're a complete fool or just plain wicked, selfish and dedicated to an alarm clock.

Beatrice   This is where I take my leave. I will go and make up John's bed. Then it's bed for me as well. John, should I call you in the morning?

John   No, I'm having a long lie-in.

Beatrice   You're not going to the advice centre?

John   If I do, it will be late afternoon.

Beatrice   Okay. (*She exits.*)

Buster   John, this country'll be a mountain for the majority of Black people and you are not much different from the rest of them except you're trying to put your idea into practice like believing every Englishman is afraid of the IRA.

Buster   Yes.

Buster   Perhaps that is the reason why you was having such a hard time.

John   Don't be ridiculous, the IRA on a trip to me, I mean I don't see what that's got to do with anything that concern it's Elaine and myself, I mean I am English but I am not white so who is afraid of who – I don't care because that is not what I mean.

Buster   A fierce statement if everything was right and proper.

John   Why is it that everything is not right and proper?

Buster   Not why, but what it is.

John   What is wrong with me?

Buster   Well, you are having a little domestic problem.

John   Yes that's true. Next to the youths, she's my biggest problem.

Buster   You are admitting that you have more than one problem.

John   Come again?

Buster   Your problem, man.

John   What should I do about her?

Buster   What is her crime?

John   Crimes? What's this, the local magistrates court?

Buster   No, tell me about the football team.

John   What football team? Man, I'm too young to have a divorce.

Buster   Man, tell me why your wife want to leave you.

John   Is me first pack my case.

Buster   So why you want to leave her?

John   I don't want to leave her.

Buster   So what is your problem? Boy, you'd better sit down in the corner and have a good cry, or find your level.

John   Did Martin Luther King used to cry?

Buster   You know about him more than me.

Doorbell.

Beatrice (*ears against door*)   I will get it.

Buster   I thought you were making up John's bed?

Beatrice   I was listening.

Buster   Have you solved John's problems?

Beatrice   No.

Doorbell – she exits.

Buster   I wonder who that is.

John   I am not going to guess.

Buster   Man, your only problem is the advice centre, take the football team with you and leave, that will give you more time to take care of your wife.

John   Where should I go? And how can I find anywhere else

Buster   Find other places the same way you find the advice centre.

John   I don't want to sell the building. I came here to talk about the problem I am having with Elaine.

Buster   The advice centre is a problem between you and your wife. You're always complaining about the pressure from the advice centre.

John   There's a lot of work to be done at the centre. How can you behave like this? Don't you realise what is happening to the young Blacks in this country? Especially in areas like these.

Buster   They all live in area like these.

John   But why?

Buster   They probably like it.

John   You hit the nail on the head.

Buster   So you're going to give up social security and police politics.

John   What politics? And what do you know about politics?

Buster   Everything, boy.

John   Don't start talking to me about your type of politics. I need everybody's support in my work.

Buster   But you'll never get everybody's support.

John   I mean in my immediate family.

*Enter **Elaine** and **Beatrice** carrying two suitcases each. They put them down, **Beatrice** beckons **Elaine** to sit, she shakes her head and leans against wall. **Beatrice** sits in easy chair.*

Elaine   You forget these.

Buster   It is time for me and Beatrice to go to bed and leave you two young lovers alone.

Elaine   Never. I will not be seen dead with him. I suppose you have poisoned your parents' mind against me with your lies.

Beatrice   No, Elaine, there is two sides to every story.

Elaine   Not his stories, they are all one-sided lies, deceit and selfishness. It all started when I said why do you have to go to court every day to bail out Black people when you are not a lawyer.

John   I can tell you are not my passport to heaven.

Elaine   He haven't seen me for the last four months and every time I see him he's fast asleep.

Buster   So how do you manage to have an argument with him?

Elaine   That's different.

Buster   In that case ignore me, I'm only here for the brandy.

Elaine   His heart, soul and body is in total confusion. How can any normal person live within four walls with that kind of person.

Beatrice   I think probably you both need a little adjustment.

John   I'm not saying anything.

Elaine   You never could.

John   Why are you only bring my clothes, what about some of the pots and pans?

Elaine   Are you complaining?

John   No, just thinking aloud.

Beatrice   What is happening between the both of you?

Buster   They are breaking up.

John   All I need is a break for a little while.

Elaine   Is that what he said?

Beatrice   What's that?

Elaine   Breaking up?

Beatrice   That's only Buster and his brandy thinks that way.

Elaine   Then when I said to him before he fall asleep is how many more court cases he have this week, he didn't even look at me much less to answer, he just grabbed his suitcase and start packing as if he was a 45 revolver go on shoot your last bullet.

John   I just need a break from all the hassle.

Elaine   Well, was that the right way to go about it?

John   I don't need an argument with anybody. I just need help and understanding from my immediate family.

Elaine   Well, you must start thinking as part of a family.

John   Didn't you say you're not going to teach at the advice centre after next Saturday?

Elaine   Yes or I might end up thinking like a man.

Beatrice   Well, it seems to me like both your problems is about work.

Buster   No, he's not fulfilling his role as a man.

Beatrice   Come on, Buster, be helpful.

Buster   Well, if he must help Black people, then there must be other ways than going to court three and four times each week like building up a Black football team to march into the First Division like the way the Jamaican battalion march into Berlin in the last world war.

John   Why do you always glorify war?

Buster   No, boy, I am just proud, are you proud of what you are doing?

John   Yes.

Buster   What have you got to show for it?

John   What have you got to show from the last world war?

Buster   My medals upstairs. You can have them when you are man enough to wear them.

John   Don't be so bloody stupid, I would not be seen dead in them.

Beatrice   Is this helping his marriage?

Buster   Beatrice, sooner or later the boy must learn the facts of life. He is killing himself in that advice centre.

Elaine   Thank you, Buster.

John (*laughs*)   I am feeling better now I know where I stand.

Buster   Have you seen sense at last?

John   Yes. As from tomorrow I'm going to live at the advice centre.

Beatrice   John, please.

Elaine   So that's why you wanted the pots and pans.

John   You always liked brother Alan more than me because he was a professional footballer.

Beatrice   John, you must not believe that. It is not true.

John   Sorry, Mother.

Beatrice   Just try and think straight, son.

John   I give up thinking. I am just going to do what I have got to do. Right, I am off.

Scene Two

John's *advice centre. Three tables with telephone on each table. Chairs and settee, blackboard, big map of the world and individual maps of Jamaica, Trinidad, Barbados, St Address book and diary on each table. Space machine.* **John** *stumbling about in the dark suitcase in hand.*

John   Look how long I've been here and I still don't know where to find the light switch, but what the rass is this? (*Stumbles over* **Rama** *and his suitcase, starts picking him up.*)

Rama   Take your hands off the general.

John   Rama, who is lock you in here?

Rama   Nobody, I got a set of keys.

John   Let me see them. (*Takes keys from him and finds light switch.*) Jane's keys.

Rama   Pick them up outside the door while I was waiting for General Atlantic or a message or a telegram. He's in the navy you know.

John   Listen, as daylight you must get out of here and go back to where you are staying.

Rama   Oh no, not now. Things are hot in South Africa at the moment. General Atlantic and myself will have to finish this operation before we can return to sheltered accommodation.

John   The first sign of daylight you must go back to the battlefield.

Rama   Yes, here is my suitcase, this is our headquarters.

Jane *enters from upstairs. In skirt and blouse, barefoot.*

Jane   What's going on?

John   What are you doing here?

Jane   Are you alright?

John   Why are you here?

Rama   She come to join the revolution.

Jane   What! I came back here and Brendan and myself had a few drinks and we fell asleep.

John   Brendan – I thought he was at his girlfriend's.

Jane   They split a couple of days ago.

John   So you are mending the split, placing him and yourself together.

Jane   You must be joking, separate rooms.

John   Those two empty room are for emergencies and now I want one of them for myself.

Jane   Oh I see, the case is yours.

John   One of them is mine, yes.

Jane   So is he your new mate? I mean are you moving in together? It is quite a surprise.

John   Why is it a surprise? We haven't been getting on very well recently.

Jane   Yes I know, but him and you.

John   Listen, here is your keys. He find them outside and let himself in here.

Jane   What for?

John   Ask him. Let him tell you what he's doing himself.

Jane   I suppose you have other things on your mind.

John   You mean my wife and I?

Jane   I am sorry.

John   She doesn't like the advice centre anymore.

Jane   She probably needs a change.

John   Well, she's welcome to do that as long as she doesn't expect me to change.

Jane   You know I am leaving as well.

John   Yes, yes, you said so before.

Key in door, **Elaine** *with two suitcases exits. Comes back with two more suitcases and exits.*

Rama   Four more soldiers.

John   So tell me something, why are you leaving?

Jane   Why ask the same old question. Ask another. Your days are too long for me, this place never closes. A nice little nine to five will do me fine at the women's centre. I am sorry about you and Elaine. It's a pity you haven't got any children, perhaps that could keep you together.

Rama   All good children will turn into soldiers when they grow up. We can't have too many of them for this South Africa operation.

John   Are you lecturing me?

Jane   No, but you are getting into a state.

John   I am in a state.

Jane   How long do you think this place will survive I mean without no GLC and all that?

John   Did you know that I actually own this building?

Jane   Yes I know, but who's going to pay the rates?

Rama   Am I supposed to be getting worried about our headquarters? Rates, I have dealings with that word before. Yes in days gone by the rates have me and General Atlantic running all over London. The English government was writing letters about rates, letters that we did not understand. Each both had a wife and six children each, but all the letters were addressed to General Atlantic or myself. Rates, after the departure of our wife and children we were bodily thrown out of our houses by men of different races and colour and with only one suitcase each we became soldiers of the streets and learn that worse fate was upon a Black brothers in South Africa. No rates did not help us to buy our houses, so why should we pay rates. We're paying rent for many years before we buy our houses.

John   Jane, have you ever heard a madder man than this?

Jane   What!

John   Carry on. No, wait a minute, General. Tell you the truth, Jane, I remember something I wanted to ask you. What I don't understand is how come the newspaper want to talk to you and not me?

Jane   You will get your turn and anyway I am involved in more than one project.

John   What did you tell them?

Jane   It wasn't like that, they were only asking political questions about South Africa.

John   Yeh, so you're in the big time like General Rama. South Africa will mad any living person.

Jane   Don't talk rubbish. We must boycott every single item from South Africa. The people of this country will have to learn through the media how wicked and barbaric it is for our Black people to live under the white minority ruling in majority regime of South Africa.

Rama   Keep up the good work. Our war in South Africa will be won with the help of all goods nations up on the hearts of all good citizens except the men who collect the rates. Step right up, be soldiers, join us to fight the men who collect the rates and the other oppressors in South Africa.

John   So tell me, Jane, have you ever met a madder man than this?

Jane   Why it seems to me that you have no heart or emotion for South Africa.

John   That's right. Cos right now my arse is on fire. When is your interview coming out?

Jane   This morning.

John   What! So it is hot, hot news. General, don't go to sleep we are going to have a busy day today.

Jane   How long have you known him?

John   Since I was a child.

Jane   Is it true what he was saying about the rates in London?

John   I don't know.

Jane   His family? Did he have daughters?

John   Yes he did have daughters. And what do you mean, if he had daughters? Sometimes I just don't understand women.

Jane   That is because you're a man.

Rama   Well, it is time to go, I have an appointment with a telephone box.

Jane   What!

Rama   With God's speed General Atlantic will be on time, so bye for now. John me soldier who is very good and John, try to keep all the soldiers together.

He exits with his suitcase.

John   What do you think about him as a madman? Go on, please tell me.

Jane   What do you think about South Africa?

John   What do you think about Black men marrying white women?

Jane   What has that got to do with South Africa?

John   My life, my wife, this place.

Jane   You see, that's why the newspaper would rather talk to me than you.

John   You must be joking. Don't you think I've got enough problems with the old and young Black people of Kilburn than to worry whether I get interviewed or not.

Jane   Sometimes your optimism opinions really pisses me off.

John   I know, that's why I'm always alone, even in marriage I am alone.

Jane   Well, you don't have to be if you give up this place.

John   The day I give up this place, that is the day I join General Rama and General Atlantic.

Jane   So you are thinking about South Africa.

John   No, I just feel a fish out of water. First we must clean up our back yards, the Blacks in this country deserve the same opportunity as anyone else.

Jane   Sometimes it is just as hard for us women as it is for Black people.

John   Then if you think seriously about your own statement you'll never leave this place for another organisation. The lowest depth any person can reach in this society is to get sentenced to a custodial prison term. The percentage of Black people who are living in this country compared with the amount of them that are in lock-up jails makes the mind boggle. The whole system is geared to put almost every Black man in jail.

Jane   No, that is not true. You can't look at Black people's life in black and white like that. There's a growing generation of young middle-class Blacks who is going up in this country that will never go to jail, well not many anyway.

John   What! Black people never allowed to carry one type of pressure like anyone else. The Black man have to carry three or four different pressure at the same time. The problems that I am dealing with is very real. The poor Black youth he not only can't find a job, he has to be on a twenty-four hours a day watch guarding himself against the police every time he goes round a corner he have to look over his shoulder because he have to be prepared to run for his life in case of misidentity. What middle-class Black? When was the last time you see any potential middle-class Black youth except in court?

Jane   All the time, on the tube and on the television and quite a few of them coming here for advice. Don't get so obsessed about Black people and prison. South Africa is the most burning situation at the moment or should I say Africa. Look at the suffering all over that continent.

John   I don't have enough strength to fight more than one political battle at the same time.

Jane   You should be ashamed of yourself. The Black people of this country needs good leadership and an international political awareness.

John   International awareness is right. The riches of this country was earned by people long before this present generation. The world came out of the earth from all over the world most of the digging was done by Black men with white bosses would you not give them any money or raw materials for their labour, and look at it now in this country where work is getting less of a burden to the Black man's back, the white bosses give him no work all because they would have to pay him for his labour. So therefore the white Englishman is almost making it impossible for the ordinary Black man to get promoted. You don't need great mathematician to work out that little puzzle for you.

Jane   Stop being so obsessed with Black people around you. Get away sometimes and start socialising with a different kind of Black youth.

John   When do I get time to socialise?

Jane   Well stop making such a rational judgements on other people's lives.

John   Am I lying?

Jane   No, but your ideas are too one-sided. Why don't you go out and liberate yourself like me?

John   It seems like we are fighting in two different wars. Jesus, I going to sleep tonight?

Jane   Sleep upstairs, or you can stay at my place. You know Elaine and myself are going away this coming weekend.

John   What about her class?

Jane   After the class.

John   Well, I might as well wait until you both leave and then go back home. Kilburn I love you, my heart bleeds for you.

Jane   Why is all this obsession about Kilburn? Get out and do something else, that's what I say. I mean how big is Kilburn anyway? How comes your political outlook are so small. I put my heart, soul and body in this place and what do I get for all my hard work on the night I lock myself out of my flat – stories everyone breaking up.

John   So what happened between Brendan and his girlfriend?

Jane   They split for what reason I do not know. Everybody seems to be splitting up.

John   Everybody?

Jane   Yes, everybody.

John   You mean all the people that you know.

Jane   What about you?

John   Me and my wife?

Jane   Yes, Elaine and you.

John   Here stood five suitcases in front of me.

Jane   Here comes the philosopher.

John   When are you leaving?

Jane   Not for a while.

John   How soon?

Jane   Soon enough. All right, take a week's notice.

John   Where are you going to take Elaine to this weekend?

Jane   Wrong again, she's taking me to one of the lonely spots up north somewhere.

John   The hardest thing about my job is to learn how to be cool. Don't matter how angry I get I must remain cool. Cucumber and cheese that's me.

Jane   What a sandwich!

Lights.

Scene Three

Lights.

Friday, same day, mid-morning. Advice centre. **John** *sitting with arms folded in suit and tie.* **Jane** *on telephone, dressed in jeans, flat shoes, pullover.* **Brendan** *in trainers, bomber jacket also on phone. No suitcases.*

Brendan (*on phone*)   Yes I will come and watch you play. Yes, please call me again next week. Cheers.

Hangs up.

Jane (*on phone*)   No, no your son don't have to live here to go away on our trips. Yes, for a day and a night. Yes, you just pay what you can afford.

She hangs up.

Brendan   Look, John, I'm really sorry, I know how you feel.

John   That's life isn't it.

Jane   Probably you two should get away together, like Elaine and myself. Nothing sexual you understand. A clean, social friendship. Explore ideas together.

Brendan   We are already exploring our ideas together. I must say I don't hate women. Do you hate women, John?

John   No, not really.

Jane   First prize for both of you.

John   I will go and get the papers.

He exits.

Brendan   What's got wrong with John and Elaine?

Jane   She wants him to be more responsible.

Brendan   What do you mean?

Jane   Like giving up this place.

Brendan   Come on, you're not serious. Is that what Elaine wants?

Jane   Yes, Brendan.

Enter **Terrence** *with suitcase, crying.*

Terrence   Please help me, miss.

Brendan   Calm down, young fellow.

Terrence   I don't know what I'm going to do if you don't help me.

Jane   We will when we find out what is happening to you.

Gives **Terrence** *hanky.* **Terrence** *takes hanky.*

Brendan   Where is your parents?

Terrence   I don't know.

Brendan   Did you just fall out of the sky?

Terrence   She doesn't like me.

Brendan   Who doesn't like you?

Terrence   Please, can I stay here. I know you put up young people who doesn't have anywhere else to go.

Jane   Not before you tell us who doesn't like you.

Terrence   I like my father, but he likes her more than me.

Brendan   Where do you live?

Terrence   I am not going back to live with him.

Jane   What is your father's name?

Terrence   Felix.

Jane   That's better. What's his address?

Jane *writes in her address book.*

Terrence   78 Fenchurch Street.

Jane   Now just calm down and tell us why you left your home.

Terrence   She hates me.

Jane   No she doesn't.

Terrence   Yes she does.

Jane   All right, why?

Terrence   I don't know. Because I am not her son.

Brendan   Whose son are you?

Terrence   Miss Pauline.

Jane   Where is she?

Terrence   I don't know. Please let me stay here until I find her.

Brendan   What's your father's telephone number?

Terrence   Please, no, he will kill me if you know as I come here for help.

Jane   Well, we will have to tell somebody that you are here.

Terrence   Yes, help me find my mother.

Jane   Does your father know where she lives?

Terrence   I don't know.

Jane   Why did she leave your father?

Terrence   They never stopped quarrelling.

Brendan   Is he living with another woman?

Terrence   Yes, she hates me.

Jane   What makes you think she hates you?

Terrence   No reason, she just do that's all. Let me stay here until I find my mother.

Jane   Not before you tell us a lot more about yourself.

Terrence   What do you want to know?

Jane   What is your name?

Terrence   Terrence.

Brendan   Terrence what?

Terrence   McCloud.

Jane   Now, Terrence, what have you done to this woman that makes her dislike you?

Terrence   Nothing, she hates my mother as well, because she is worried my mother is going to come back home. She's always telling my father how my mother is no good.

Brendan   Does he agree with her?

Terrence   Sometimes.

Jane   We will have to tell your father that you are here.

Terrence   No, please.

Brendan   Or the police, they will find your mother.

Terrence   No the police will only put me into council care.

Jane   No they won't.

Terrence   Yes they will. That's what happens to most of my friends.

Jane   You are creating a big problem for us.

Terrence   Sorry, miss.

Jane   You might even get us into trouble.

Terrence   No, miss, I'll behave myself, I promise.

Jane   You can only stay here for a day until we talk to your father.

Terrence   No, miss, please talk to my mother.

Brendan   Well, we can't find your mother until we talk to your father.

Terrence All right, but please don't tell him I'm staying here.

Jane Terrence, this is no place for a young boy like yourself.

Brendan Have you ever been in trouble with the police?

Terrence No.

Jane What about school?

Terrence When I find my mother I will go back.

Enter **John**.

John Terrence, what are you doing here?

Terrence I run away from home, sa.

John Does Felix know you are here?

Terrence No, sa.

Jane He wants to stay until he finds his mother.

John Don't be daft, I will call Felix.

Terrence Please no, his woman doesn't like me.

John Where is your mother?

Terrence I don't know, but must find her.

John Jane, will you take him home?

Jane If he will come with me.

John Of course he will. Go and sit down, Terrence, while I phone Felix.

Terrence They are not there. He's going to Southend with her.

John When did they go?

Terrence Yesterday.

John When are they coming back?

Terrence Tomorrow.

John Have you got your keys?

Terrence Yes.

Jane You're not going to send him back to stay there on his own, are you?

Brendan Why don't you let him stay here until tomorrow.

John All right, take him and his case upstairs.

Brend Okay. Come on, Terrence.

John And you don't know where your mother Pauline is?

Terrence   No, sa, but I must find her.

John   All right, I'll find her for you.

Terrence   Thanks.

Exit **Brendan** *and* **Terrence**.

Jane   The paper, my interview! What did they say?

John   You are going to like it.

Jane   Let me see it. Yes, that's the only way to bring South Africa to its knees. (*She is reading newspaper quickly.*) Photograph as well. Yes I do like it. Now, wait a minute I didn't say that.

John   What's that?

Jane   That half the Houses of Parliament should be Black before sanction would work against South Africa.

John   Sounds good to me.

Jane   Yes, but it is not practical.

John   Any suggestion is good news for the Blacks.

Jane   Thank God they agree with me.

John   Where did Pauline say she was going to live? (*He looks in diary.*) Yes, here it is, 62 Feat Street and no phone number. Will you go and see her for me and tell her to come and fetch Terrence.

Jane   Sure. What is she like?

John   A normal Black woman who falls in love with another man.

Jane   Does he love her?

John   I don't know.

Jane   Poor Terrence.

John   Yes, the children always come out worse in every broken marriage.

Jane   What is the name of the other man?

John   Peter I think.

Jane   Will he look after Terrence?

John   He will have to.

Jane   Should I go and see her now?

John   Yes, when you're ready.

Jane   Hope he's a nice man. Terrence seems such a nice boy. He deserves a nice home.

John   Let's hope it works out for him.

Jane   I am off then. What is the address again?

John   62 Feat Street. (*She writes this on a piece of paper.*) And her name is Pauline.

Jane   Yeh sure, see you later.

John   Yeh.

Jane *exits.* **John** *dials phone.*

John   Hello, Elaine. Are you coming in this morning for your wages? *He listens.* I know it is your last class. (*He listens.*) Yes, I also know you are going away with Jane. Yes, I'm going to move back home when you leave. Anything else? Okay. Bye. (*He hangs up.*) The world is getting smaller and smaller every day.

Enter **Brendan** *amd* **Terrence***.*

Terrence   Can I play the space machine?

John   Sure.

Terrence   Thanks.

John   Jane is going to find your mother.

Terrence   Really, do you know where she is?

John   We will soon find out. And she never come and visited you since she left?

Terrence   No, but she said after divorce I could come and live with her.

John   When did she leave?

Terrence   Last week.

Brendan   And he is already living with another woman?

Terrence   She was there before my mother left.

Brendan   Does your mother have a boyfriend?

Terrence   No, not really. She love my father but he don't believe her.

John   All right Terrence, go and play the machine.

Terrence *plays on machine.*

Enter **Leonard***,* **Charkey** *and* **Denzil** *playing football.*

Charkey   Over here, Denzil.

John   All right, cut it out.

They stop playing football.

Brendan   I hope you'll put as much effort in the match on Sunday.

Charkey   It will be a walkover.

Denzil   Have you picked the team yet?

Brendan   Yes, you're playing in the middle.

Denzil   Come on, man, you can't be serious. I'm the best centre-forward this team ever had.

Brendan   You haven't scored a goal since I take over the training.

Denzil   That's because nobody doesn't pass the ball to me.

Brendan   Why should they?

Leonard   I will pass the ball to him.

Brendan   Who said you're playing.

Leonard   Me. I man must play.

Brendan   I have eleven other players that is far superior to you lot.

Denzil   We are no lot. Lot wife turned into a pillar of salt.

Charkey   So you feel us dread is not good enough to win the match.

Brendan   I know you are not.

Leonard   John, talk to his Irish trainer about us dread.

John   He is the boss. Where is the rest of the team?

Charkey   We are your most faithful customer. Where would this place be without the pleasure of our company.

Denzil   We three are the champions of everything around here.

Charkey   Watch this heavy movement.

Denzil and **Charkey** *start playing football.*

John   I am not impressed.

Leonard   Why should you? You have other things on your mind.

Brendan   Where did you get your information?

Charkey   We know everything.

Denzil   Let's get this youth off the machine.

John   Leave him alone.

Leonard   Why?

John   Because I said so.

Enter **Rama**.

Rama   Oh John, my boy, General Atlantic have made great achievement, he's now in control of the American navy. (*Moves across in front of map.*) Right, gather round me young soldiers.

Brendan   What did you say about the navy, colonel?

Rama (*loudly*)   General!

Terrence *stops playing the machine.*

Leonard   This look like a real forward movement.

Denzil   Yes, could be.

Charkey   A madman.

Denzil *amd* **Charkey** *gather round* **Rama**. **Terrence** *joins them.* **John** *sits down.*
Brendan *stands back smiling.*

Charkey   Yes, General show us your movements.

Denzil   Yes man, let me see your diplomatic style.

Rama   Yes indeed.

Brendan *laughs.*

Leonard   Just watch yourself, trainer.

John   General, before you start, let me tell you something.

Rama   Go ahead, John my boy.

John   I am serious.

Rama   I know, I know, please continue.

John   I am tired.

Rama   I am sorry.

John   Man, listen to me, don't get too mad in here today.

Charkey   He's a wise man to be mad, he ain't got no problem.

John   Shut up you little half-hearted youth. Brendan, do you enjoy working with
these people? Can you compare our problems with anyone else?

Rama   John, my boy, our problems are about to be over.

Brendan   It is just a funny day that's all.

John   Rama, this place is for young people, it is here for the sole purpose to stop
them from going to prison and it is supposed to be a peaceful resting home. It is not
for a mad old man like yourself.

Uproar between **Charkey,** **Leonard** *and* **Denzil.**

Charkey   How can you say that?

Leonard   I mean, you wicked, the man is nice.

Denzil   Carry on, General.

Terrence *goes back to machine.*

Brendan (*laughs*)   It is a funny day.

Rama   No, young one, listen to the great progress we have made in eliminating the oppressors of South Africa. (*He takes* **Terrence** *by hand and takes him to the map. Everyone else watches in silence.*) General Atlantic is only one day away this point, (*he points his finger*) Cape Town, Africa, his destination. We are standing by for a major battle.

Shirley *enters – hysterical, two suitcases, three or four shopping bags.*

Shirley   Johnny hit me. I told him a hundred times if you ever hit me I'm going to leave him. No police on judge will let him get away with this wickedness.

Denzil   Yes, Miss B, calm down.

Shirley   I can't. I need a bed for tonight. I got nowhere to go.

Rama   Oh come with me.

Shirley   Shut up, old man.

John   Rama, you're not going to contact General Atlantic.

Rama   Oh yes I must.

Terrence *goes back to machine.* **Rama** *exits.*

John   Now, Shirley, what's the problem?

Charkey, **Denzil** *and* **Leonard** *go over to the machine. Watching* **Terrence**.

Shirley   Can I stay here for a while, I mean just for today and tonight. I will make up my mind what to do tomorrow.

John   No, we will find somewhere else for you to go.

Shirley   Could you, John?

She looks at **Brendan**.

John   It's all right, Brendan works here. Just tell us what happened.

Brendan   Please, we're here to help you. Are you badly hurt?

Shirley   No, just a few bruised ribs.

Brendan   Do you want to go to the hospital?

Shirley   No, no I'll be alright. I will see what happens tomorrow.

John   Why did he hit you?

Shirley   Well, we've been saving up for a carpet and some wallpaper. Christ almighty, the place is so damp. Every two months the wallpaper start peeling off the wall, water is coming through the roof and messing up the carpet need a new piece of carpet for a long, long time. Anyway him take the £150 and say he was going to buy the wallpaper and the piece of carpet we been looking at in the shop window for a month.

John   And he didn't buy the carpet, and he came home drunk and hit you.

Shirley   Yes that's right

Brendan   Does he gamble?

Shirley   I don't know what he does with all that money.

Brendan   He's not supposed to hit you and get away with it.

John   Where is he now?

Shirley   Sleeping.

Brendan   Are you prepared to leave him?

Shirley   Yes, I want to live alone. I find myself a job.

Brendan   We will help you, I promise you.

John   Right. I think I'd better talk to Alison or my brother.

Brendan   Yes, she have a few vacancies.

John   We are going to try and get you fixed up in a nice private hostel for women like yourself.

Shirley   Are they all Black women?

Brendan   No.

John   Mind you, it's not permanent, just temporary.

Shirley   Thank you, John.

John   While you are there you can make up your mind if you want to go back to your old man or not.

Shirley   No, no after eight years it's over.

John   Right, I will call Alison. (*Dials.*) Hello, Alison, yes thanks, yes I have got a little Miss Shirley for you. Thanks, I'm sending her over in a minicab. (**John** *writes in diary. Dials.*) Yes, John, Shirley, okay, she'll wait outside.

Shirley   Let me know how you get on.

Lights.

Act Two

Scene One

Lights.

Advice centre, same day, lunchtime, **Denzil**, **Charkey** *and* **Leonard** *drinking Coca-Cola and eating hamburgers,* **John** *and* **Brendan** *sitting at their tables.*

Denzil   You have any good reason why we should not hate every white man?

Brendan   I am not here as your political object. Football is what I'm here to teach you and keep you away from the arms of the law.

John   Tell me something, don't you guys have any ambition? Is every single one of you going to let me down?

Denzil   What do you mean, mass P?

John   The football that you are playing, it is there to stimulate your head and make you think of doing something better with your lives.

Leonard   Man having no proper direction in life can only be blamed on the political situation, so we must try and make everyone understand the situation.

John   So what do you think I'm trying to do all day?

Brendan   Look, I also do a lot of work in this office in trying to solve other people's problems.

John   And he is doing a good job as well.

Charkey   Nobody is disputing that he's not a hard worker.

Brendan   I am not like one of your white Englishman, I just had boiled bacon and cabbage for lunch.

Denzil   All right, Brendan, we will finish this discussion another day.

Enter **Terrence** *with two cups of tea for* **Brendan** *and* **John**.

Brendan   And I have good news for all of you.

Denzil   Yes, what's that?

Brendan   All three of you will be playing up front next week if you can prove to me that you are willing to score goals.

Charkey   And we are going to win the cup.

Terrence   I can play football.

Denzil   Well let's see you then.

Denzil, **Charkey**, **Leonard**, **Terrence** *start playing football. Enter* **Elaine** *and* **Jane**.

Elaine   Hello, boys.

All four boys stop playing football and say hello.

Jane   She is not there, sorry, Terrence.

Terrence   Thanks for trying.

John   My God, how many more problems can this place cope with? When will I find any peace of mind? How can I cope with the problem of a young kid like this?

Brendan   I know what will do, let's take Terrence over the park for a game of football.

Denzil   What are we waiting for.

Leonard   Let's go.

Exit **Denzil, Charkey, Terrence** *and* **Leonard**.

Elaine   Hello, John. My last lesson tomorrow.

John   Yes, I know.

Jane   I have to go and meet Dennis Pritchard from the women's centre, we're organising a match in support of Winnie and Nelson Mandela so Elaine I will see you later. I am sure you and John have lots to talk about. Hope you find somewhere nice for Terrence. Bye.

Elaine   Yes, later.

Jane *exits.*

Elaine   So you are still hanging on to this place.

John   Yes, it's tough but it gives me satisfaction.

Elaine   Why don't you give up and do something else. Don't you see everybody is leaving. How long do you think Brendan will be able to stick around?

John   Look at this. (*Shows her papers.*) Another six Black youths is going to go to jail if I don't rescue them. Where am I going to find room to put them?

Elaine   For heaven's sake, can't you see you're not making any progress.

John   You know, when I was younger, I mean very young, I mean when I first start reading about the Black movement in America . . .

Enter **Rama**.

Rama   John, John my boy, General Atlantic have landed.

John   Please go away, just for a little while, so I can talk to my wife, eh general.

Rama   We have captured South Africa.

Elaine   Good for you.

Rama   Yes the battle is still raging thick and fast, but we are winning, they're on the run, yes I must get back to my post.

Exit **Rama**.

Elaine   How much longer have you got, John?

John   For what?

Elaine   I mean before you're completely freaked out?

John   All my life.

Elaine   Some life. You're not going to be able to support yourself, not for much longer.

John   That's what you think. Are you a lesbian?

Elaine   No, for God's sake, why?

Joh   So why are you going away with Jane?

Elaine   Is she lesbian?

John   I don't know.

Elaine   We are going away together on women's business. What were you saying? You mentioned America.

John   Why are you tormenting me? You're leaving me alone to run this place. I don't remember saying anything about America. Oh forget it.

Elaine   You see, you're losing your concentration. Our marriage would work out fine if you would give up this place and go back to doing what you were doing before. Who is going to finance you? You already have a second mortgage on this place.

John   You have it all worked out, haven't you?

Elaine   Yes, give up and write a book and let the government do its own dirty work. I would stand by you if you go on the streets and start preaching hate against South Africa, or something like that. When are you going to court about the six youths in custody? (*She is looking at papers.*)

John   Monday. You want to come with me.

Elaine   I am finished with this place, John. There is no promotion of progress in it for either of us, just more and more problems.

Enter **Buster** *and* **Beatrice**.

Buster   Hello, John. We are worried.

John   Hi, Mum.

Buster   Glad to see you, Elaine.

Elaine   Yes, very nice to see you.

Buster   Have you changed your mind?

Elaine   No.

Buster   Sorry to hear that, I must admit that I have changed my mind. If this is what he wants to do, we will stand by him.

Beatrice   Yes, that's right, son. And your brother sends his love.

Elaine   Well, well. Dear John live to fit another day.

John   I will get your wages, Elaine. (*He open safe.*) Oh God, it's empty.

Buster   What empty?

John   Everything.

Beatrice   You mean you have been robbed?

Elaine   I am not surprised.

John   I will have to call the police this time.

Elaine   While you're at it, you might as well get the ambulance for yourself.

Buster   How much money was it, John?

John   Eight, nine hundred pounds.

Beatrice   Probably it is time to give up and come back home and start all over again.

Buster   Leave him, Beatrice.

Elaine   Just forget about my wages, I'm sorry.

Beatrice   Well, go ahead and call the police.

Elaine   He wouldn't call the police, he's afraid they would come and take away one of his beloved youths.

John   There seems to be a calculated hate trip going against me.

Buster   It seems like nobody is not supposed to do a job like this for more than six months.

Elaine   Oh I know that, I have learned my lesson several times over.

Beatrice   Poor John.

John   I really am truly would just like to sit down and have a good cry.

Beatrice   Tears from the big man like you, son?

Buster   Well, if you wants to cry let him cry

Elaine   The whole idea in keeping this advice centre open is a sick joke.

John   Haven't you had enough bones for one day? What more do you want. My mother and father as well?

Elaine   My God, what a wicked, selfish man.

Buster   When are you two going to stop bickering with each other and get on with the little love that you have got between you.

Elaine   God knows I've tried.

John   What you try to do except to send me to an early grave.

Elaine   You mean that is what you've been trying to do to me, but you will probably run out of steam before you succeed.

Buster   Come, Beatrice, let's leave them to get on with it.

Beatrice   No, Buster, let's just try once more. What about the police, are you going to call them?

John   I need to talk to Brendan and some of the boys before I do anything else. Dad, can you put up a young boy for me? It will only be for a few days until I sort it out between him and his parents.

Beatrice   Ask Beatrice. She's the one who will have to feed him.

Beatrice   Anything you say, son.

John   Thanks. I'll bring him over later this evening or tomorrow morning.

Beatrice   What about you, son, where are you living?

John   I am all right. I am busy at the moment. My problem will sort itself out in a little while.

Buster   Well, John, I would do anything for you but I'm not giving you no more money to keep this place going.

Beatrice   Why can't you get a proper government grant to finance this place?

Buster   Man, you cannot go on forever with a begging bowl hoping that rich Black business men will continue to support you.

Elaine   He'll never get enough money together to run this place and support himself.

Beatrice   What a shame.

John   Well, here we go again, another crisis on top of my head.

Elaine   Well, for God's sake, get it off your head and come home before it is too late.

Beatrice   Just listen to those sweet, nice words, son.

Buster   He's not listening, he's in a trance.

John   No, I am not ready to flee this death trap not until the Black youths in and around here begun to get a job instead of sentence to youth custody. Tell me something, do you people really know what is going on?

Beatrice   Maybe not as much as you, but we do have our own beliefs.

Buster   What kind of life is this, you own these houses and you can't find a bed in them to rest your head. Is your wife got to put you up.

Elaine   No please, that's all right.

John   What you want me to do, go around with a guilty conscience in my heart?

Buster   Why don't you throw out the young rogues and clean up the place and make a home out of it for you and your wife and sell the other one.

Elaine   I don't want to live here.

John   Listen all of you, leave, I've got things to sort out.

Beatrice   Whatever you say, son. Come, Buster, let's go. Don't forget your brother is coming to see you.

John   Yes thanks.

Elaine   I am going home. Beatrice, I will come and see you before I go away for the weekend.

Beatrice   Yes, alright.

Exit **Elaine**.

Buster   John, sometimes you talk to us as if we are your enemy.

John   Please leave.

Beatrice   Yes, come, Buster.

Buster   Right, it's your life.

John   Nine hundred pounds. That money could keep this place going for another month. (*Closes his eyes. Very sad.*)

Buster   It's your life, son. Come, Beatrice, let's leave him.

Beatrice   Just come home when you're ready, son.

Exit **Beatrice** *and* **Buster**. **John** *dials*.

John   Hello, Raymond, it's John, they done me in again. The safe didn't help. Yeh, nine hundred pounds. (**John** *listens*.) I expect another six youths by next week. (**John** *listens*.) I am dying to have a good joke like I laugh all the way to the bank. Yes, Raymond, you have to have a sense of humour in times like these. Okay, see you soon. (*He dials, line engaged. He dials.*)

Enter **Shirley**.

Shirley   Hello, John. Oh, I thank you very much, yes it is a nice place.

John *hangs up phone*.

John   You like it.

Shirley   Oh, yes everyone is so friendly including the lady who is in charge.

John   Good, I am pleased. Somebody has robbed my safe. I can't understand it, I'm the only one who's got a key.

Shirley   What do you mean? Some of these wicked youths rob a good man like you, why men so wicked?

John   Not every woman is an angel.

Shirley   Woman doesn't know how to break into safes.

John   Don't be daft.

Shirley   I suppose you are right. So sorry, John, really sorry. I am going to work for the railway again. I phoned my old supervisor and she said I could have my old job again. Isn't that good news.

John   Yes, very good news.

Shirley   Is that man come in here looking for me?

John   No, it's not four hours since you left him.

Shirley   You see, he doesn't care anything about me.

John   Are you thinking about him?

Shirley   Yes, a little. If he didn't drink so much it would probably work out for the both of us.

John   Who knows, you might get back together sooner or later.

Shirley   No, he shouldn't have hit me. Don't matter how drunk he was. Still, I might look in on him one day. Don't know when that day will be, but I might just go back, just to look at the flat.

John   When are you thinking of going back? We don't want to have any more meetings now do we?

Shirley   Like I said, I don't know when that day will be, but thank God I feel strong enough to look after myself.

John   When do you expect to start your new job?

Shirley   I am going to see her on Monday, so if God spare my life, not next week but the other week.

John   Good, so forget your old man for a while.

Shirley   Yes I'm going to band my belly against him. I was hoping that you would let me have a little spare cash until I get my first pay packet, but Lord Jesus be merciful, they have robbed you.

John   Yes, never mind. How much do you need?

Shirley   Not much, but do you know how long the social security take to pay when you change your circumstances.

John   Yes, I understand. I haven't got much. You realise that everything is crashing down around me.

Shirley   John, if I lay a hand on the man who rob your safe I would kill him.

John   Take it easy. Probably it is a woman who take the money.

Shirley   Is what you telling me?

John   Anyway, let's get back to your problem.

Shirley   Well, I seem to be having everything free where I am living, but I need a little extra, just in case for some emergency.

John   Twenty-five pounds enough?

Shirley   Yes, more than enough. I didn't expect you would be so generous.

John   No, that's all right. Pay me back when you have it, if I am still here.

Shirley   Why, where are you going? I hope everything is all right with you. (**John** *gives her £25 from his wallet.*) I am sorry about your safe, thank you.

John   It is a small world, I will soon find out who robbed the safe.

Shirley *counts the money.*

Shirley   Thanks, this is very nice of you.

John   No problem.

Lights.

Scene Two

Lights.

Advice centre. Saturday morning. **Jane** *sitting on table,* **Elaine** *sitting on chair. Both very relaxed.*

Jane   Well, what do you think?

Elaine   Let him think what he likes.

Jane   I am leaving, but at the same time I wouldn't like to hurt him.

Elaine   He's already hurt.

Jane   The robbery from the safe was the last straw.

Elaine   It happened before.

Jane   You think he's jealous about us going away together?

Elaine   I told you before, I don't care, because there is nothing for him to be jealous about.

Jane   Maybe we're leaving at the wrong time.

Elaine   Perhaps, but it is no use flogging a dead horse.

Jane   Well we might as well stay for the final curtain.

Elaine   Has he talked to you about his new training scheme?

Jane   No, not really. I know about the application.

Elaine   Well, he might just get the training scheme off the ground, but there'll be no job for us.

Jane   Well, good for him.

Elaine   He's too soft towards men. Wish he was like that with women.

Jane   Is that why you're leaving him?

Elaine   No, I'm not leaving him. I just need a change of direction, That's all.

Jane   I stick around longer than I thought I would.

Elaine   It is different for me. Maybe I will have to spend the rest of my life with him.

Jane   I see. Perhaps we should continue with our present job and see what happens to his training regime.

Elaine   He won't be able to continue paying your salary for much longer.

Jane   Oh, I'm not doing it for the money. I am getting more and more involved with the Women's Movement.

Elaine   I can't make up my mind which way to turn.

Jane   Maybe you just want to settle down and have a private life with John.

Elaine   I don't know.

Jane   You must find out before it is too late.

Elaine   Yes I am playing everything by ear at the moment. Do you like Brendan?

Jane   Yes, but only as a friend.

Elaine   That kind of relationship never worked for me.

Jane   Oh, I have lots of men friends.

Elaine   I know, I always wonder about that.

Jane   I'll choose one of them when I'm ready to have a baby.

Elaine   I thought you was different.

Jane   Oh did you.

Elaine   Sorry.

Jane   Don't be, do you fancy me?

Elaine   I like you.

Jane   Me too. You think we should share a flat together if it doesn't work out for John and yourself?

Elaine   I would like to have a baby before I do that.

Jane   I am a feminist. I am in love with women, that's all.

Elaine   How do you manage to do that?

Jane   Aren't you?

Elaine   Well, not in love.

Jane   Haven't you ever kissed another woman?

Elaine   Yes.

Jane   I mean passionately.

Elaine   No.

Jane   Maybe you should try it with me.

Elaine   Have you tried it before?

Jane   No, but we could learn together.

Elaine   When I get tired of men penetrating my body that is probably what I will do with other women in my spare time.

Jane   You think I should get married and learn the hard way as well?

Elaine   It could be what you need.

Jane   Yes, maybe. (*They laugh.*) What are we going to do about John?

Elaine   Let's stick around together and find out. Are you a lesbian?

Jane   No I am not. Quite often I fancy going to bed with a man.

Elaine   Are you a virgin?

Jane   No. I just don't sleep around anymore.

Enter **Brendan** *from upstairs.*

Brendan   Morning, what a shame about the robbery. Now he's not sure if he did put the money in the safe.

Jane   Sadness always seems to bring people together more closely.

Brendan   What do you mean?

Jane   Well, I might stay on for a while longer.

Brendan   John would be pleased. What about you, Elaine?

*

Charkey   Yes, the kid is a good footballer. Makes a good winner.

Denzil   What about this lesson on Caribbean history, Miss Elaine?

Leonard   Where is the rest of them?

Jane   We don't live here.

Brendan   They are away.

Charkey   With the money from the safe.

Brendan   Yes, where are they? They should be back early this morning.

Denzil   They seem to spend all their lives in the minibus.

Jane   Don't start getting any ideas, they are not thieves.

Brendan   They are always late for football training.

Denzil   Maybe it is a blessing that the money has gone missing from the safe.

Elaine   Don't you guys have girlfriends?

Denzil   Yes, late at night until the early hours of the morning.

Jane   So what happens to them during the day?

Leonard   They play silly little games with each other.

Elaine   I'm giving no more lessons to you people.

Charkey   Well, you promised that you was going to tell us a little about the Jamaican history.

Denzil   And the Rasta movement and all that.

Elaine   I don't know anything about Rasta.

Leonard   What! This is the only history about Jamaica.

Charkey   Bob Marley.

Leonard   He was a Rasta.

Denzil   So who was in control before Marcus Garvey?

Charkey   No one man. He was the first.

Leonard   Well, I heard Captain Morgan was once the governor before him.

Charkey   Yes, but he was in charge?

Leonard   Yes, that's a different kettle of fish.

---

* Due to the age and scarcity of the original manuscripts, this section of the playtext has unfortunately been lost to time.

Jane Will you all stop taking the piss and find a way to put the money back into the safe before John calls the police.

Denzil Is he going to call the police?

Elaine Yes, when he sees sense.

Brendan Good. It is about time some of these yobs pay for their crimes around here.

Denzil Listen, man, if you want to continue to be our trainer and work in the office don't talk or think about the police.

Charkey Or we will cut our hair and join the police.

Brendan I don't like the police, but there comes a time when we need them.

Leonard Cut out this police talk and let's talk about the Bible.

Denzil And pray for the wicked thief to return the money to the safe.

Brendan You seem to find the whole situation quite amusing.

Denzil No man, very serious.

Leonard So serious that if we find out who done the thieving we'll make a citizen's arrest ourself.

Brendan How can long can John survive?

Jane Yes, Elaine, with the both of us leaving it seems a sad waste of energy for John to continue in the present situation.

Denzil Don't talk about him as if he's dead.

Leonard So tell me something, how many youths live here now?

Jane Eight, sometimes ten.

Denzil Well, the three of us will move back in again to keep our eyes on the safe for John.

Elaine Yes if you don't mind being a guard for an empty safe. I now begun to feel sorry for John.

Brendan I have a vision that I could build a West Indian football team capable of taking on the best in the Southern League and who knows with a little help from our friends, we would probably make it to the league in a few years.

Leonard You hear that, Charkey?

Charkey What do you think, Denzil?

Denzil Man, it is only a dream to keep us confused. Black people always have to put up with more disappointment than any other nation or group of people.

Leonard Yes, in the past we have always lose our leaders before they could do any proper work for us Blacks. Not many have ever risen above the hand-to-mouth brigade.

Charkey   Yes because as soon as they reach any kind of heights, the white man chop them down with the help of jealous Black people.

Denzil   We must ignore these people and reach for higher heights.

Leonard   What I don't understand is how any man could be so wicked to come in here and rob the safe.

Elaine   And there is no GLC to bail John out of trouble this time.

Charkey   Yes I can see. Old Ken Livingstone coming back to fight for us Blacks. Boy oh boy, John must be in a sad state of mind for all the hard work he put into this place.

Denzil   Well, the only thing he can do is to sell the houses to the council and let them is that the running of the centre.

Brendan   Well, since you Rastas are getting so intellectual why don't you nominate yourself as Rasta candidates to run in the local elections.

Jane   Why stop at one candidate?

Elaine   Rasta running the town hall? With Ken Livingstone in the chair, what a scream that would be.

Charkey   Now I can see why John employ you, are a bloody genius, Brendan.

Leonard   Yes, man, him learn from the Englishman in Northern Ireland.

Brendan   I can see I am going to lose some very good footballers.

Charkey   You're right. Football is so for kids like Terrence who will probably make it to one of the First Division teams.

Denzil   Truth and justice would be the name of the game when we run the council with the Bible.

John *enters with three yards of rope over his shoulder, accompanied by* **Terrence***.*

John   Any news on who thiefed the money?

Denzil   Not yet, but we will find out.

John   Okay. Terrence, go and get your case.

Exit **Terrence***.*

John   Brendan, will take you over to my parents for me. Here is the address. (*Gives* **Brendan** *piece of paper.*)

Brendan   Yes, sure.

John   Elaine, what you and Jane still doing here? I thought you would be half way up the motorway on your special weekend.

Elaine   Well, I was waiting to take the class, but it seems like nobody else is going to turn up.

John   I thought they would be back from the trip by now, so that's it then. Jane, don't bother to turn up next week as it is your last week and I don't have enough money to pay you.

Jane   Oh my God. You don't think I was working here for the money do you? I hope I will be remembered for better things than money.

Elaine   Jane and I was thinking of staying on for a bit longer until you get yourself straightened out with the training scheme.

John   Thank you, but there is no need for you to be so concerned.

Elaine   That is not much considering the situation.

Jane   Yes, that's right.

John   Well, if you two can pick up from where you left off when you come back that would be useful.

Elaine   So we'll see you when we get back. Sorry about the class.

Denzil   The Black man get let down again.

Jane   Right, see you next week. Hope you sort out the money problem.

John   Yeh, I will.

Enter **Terrence**.

Brendan   Okay. young fellow, let's go.

Jane   Would you like a lift, Brendan?

Brendan   Yes, thanks.

Terrence   Sir, thank you very much. I will come and visit you every day when I'm not at school.

John   Thanks. Just remember what I tell you, it is only for a little while. We can't find your mother so you'll have to go home to your father.

Terrence   Yes, I know.

John   Good boy.

Charkey   Mannersable little fellow.

Leonard   Yes, man.

Terrence *smiles*.

Brendan   See you over the weekend, John. Must get myself ready for the match.

John   Hope you win.

Brendan   We have to.

Exit **Elaine**, **Jane**, **Brendan** *and* **Terrence**.

John *sits on table and starts making hangman noose with rope.*

Denzil   Yes, we're going to win the cup.

Charkey   Brother John, I see vengeance in your eyes and heart.

Leonard   Never see you as deep as this before.

John   Is one of the three of you going to tell me who take the money from the safe? All of you know every thief in Kilburn.

Charkey   We are looking at the rope in your hand.

John *undoes hangman noose, gets ball of string and screwdriver from drawer, sits down and starts making a proper hangman noose.*

Leonard   Are you planning to hang somebody?

John   No, man. You see, I just don't like the hangman noose so I'm making sure I am looking at it all the time. That way I will make no mistake. So if anybody want to use it and hang themselves that is their business.

Denzil   Those wisdom is part of a Rasta doctrine.

Leonard   So, brother John, all three of us is clean, man.

Charkey   And you come close in saying is one of us rob your safe.

Denzil   Us who was clean when we first volunteer to help you is still clean. Our thought is not rest with the vanity of money. The Lord work wonders in many different ways.

Leonard   Are you thinking about what Brendan said this morning?

Denzil   What else?

John   Does Brendan know who robbed my safe?

Denzil   He didn't tell us, man.

Leonard   The wisdom of life is not with death until the end.

Charkey   And we have a long way to go before they stop hanging people in England for thieving.

Denzil   Not that I blame you, brother John, for carrying such wicked thoughts in your heart. Yes, they done the dirty on you, man, it's about time we stop the white man from laughing at those that try to help us Black youths.

Leonard   So leave this scene and do something else.

Denzil   We would like you to run in the next local election.

Charkey   Yes, man, and represent us from the town hall.

Denzil   Or we are going to leave this thing and get more involved with their own local scene.

Leonard   What is this place? Hotel, hostel, advice centre or a place where anybody could walk in and rob the safe.

John   Are you seriously asking me to go and knock on white people's door and ask them to vote for me?

Denzil   Yes, why not.

Charkey   If we can't beat them, then we must join them.

John   You want me to support this wicked system against Black people?

Leonard   No man, change it when you get to the town hall.

Denzil   And instead of waiting on them government people to give you money to run this place, you will become the person who will be handing out the money.

Leonard   So, brother John, put away the hangman noose for ever and let us put our sight on a higher vision.

John   I am determined to find out who rob the safe.

Charkey   Then what? Maybe all the money's already been spent.

John   Do you know some things that I don't know, Charkey?

Charkey   Man, ask me a proper question.

Denzil   Brother John, you know we're against thieving and violence. You got to help yourself before you can help others. We need you to represent us in the town hall.

Charkey   This hangman noose is making me nervous.

John   Why are you getting hot under the collar?

Charkey   Yes in case you do something stupid.

Denzil   Are we persuading you?

John   Yes, carry on. I will put away the hangman noose for a while.

Denzil   For ever, man.

John (*he puts the hangman noose on the table*)   Yes, talk to me and tell me how to put the nine hundred pounds back in the safe to keep this place going for another week or two.

Charkey   What nine hundred pounds is nothing. Why should you get yourself in trouble for peanuts.

John   Peanuts? That money is life and death for some people.

Leonard   Don't forget your wife, mother and father and those two houses that you put together to make up this place that you called advice centre belongs to you.

Charkey   So convert them back into single houses, some of them and find another way to help Black people.

Denzil   Local politics, that should be your next move.

John   Today's Saturday, what is some kid coming here and need help, what will I do for money?

Denzil   Man, let another government department deal with this situation, it is a government job to find a place for people to live.

John   Which government ever do that for poor Black people?

Denzil   That's why you must get to the town hall and become a part of the machine that will change the system and allow truth and justice to practise for all.

Leonard   Hallelujah!

Denzil   Praise the Lord!

Leonard   Praise the Lord!

Charkey   Praise the Lord!

Denzil   Praise the Lord

Leonard   Praise the Lord!

John   Praise the Lord yes, gentlemen.

Denzil   Praise the Lord!

John   Amen.

Rama *enters.*

Rama (*heavy breathing almost out of breath*)   John General Atlantic is now flying home for a more detailed map study. He'll be coming here at headquarters. As you can see, he is flying so he is negotiating with the Royal Air Force for some very fast low-flying bombers, so please help me to collect all the maps on South Africa, he will need to study them very carefully.

John   Has he lost the battle?

Rama   No, he is winning.

Denzil   Why is he called General Atlantic and not General Caribbean?

Rama   Because there are more ships in the Atlantic.

Charkey   Good answer.

Leonard   Yes, him make point.

John   So how many months do you think he will need?

Rama   Oh, many, because the one that he chooses will have to be in minute details for the airports to finish the war.

John   Right, we'll see what we can do when he arrives. Anything else?

Rama   No, I will return to my post and await his arrival.

He exits.

John   So I am not worthy of running my own place anymore.

Denzil No man, look at it this way. This is a public place for lots of different things.

Leonard Yes that's right.

Charkey Not, unless John convert this building back into private dwellings.

Denzil And I can't see John doing that.

John When did you get the idea about politics?

Denzil Brendan said why don't we go into local politics and we immediately looked at each other and we know it was you.

John Thank you. Does Brendan know you were going to talk to me?

Denzil No, but he will soon find out. Man, the same way you give up DJing, is the same way you must give up this place and move into a more powerful position which will bring a better fulfilment out of life for all of us. Man, we will support you until you win the election and beyond. The more powerful you get, the more smaller the world becomes.

Leonard And that way you can solve many more problems for Black people.

Denzil Praise the Lord!

Charkey Praise the Lord!

Leonard Praise the Lord!

John Amen.

Denzil Yes, man, go there and spread the political news like the preacher man and make them know that we wanted equality from a political point of view because if they are not careful the only place where true equality is going to practise in this country is in prison.

Leonard And that cannot be a good thing for the betterment of this country

Charkey Say something, brother John.

John Praise the Lord!

Charkey Movements.

Denzil I didn't know until I was ill in hospital that I could like people who I hate. I used to lay there feeling sad for not able to walk around Piccadilly and Oxford Street when I feel like it so I for one will canvas for you day and night amongst white people.

Leonard And so will the rest of us with only a little time for sleeping.

John I must admit you guys are getting at me. Probably time has come for me to bury the hangman noose.

Denzil Man, get into the power game and give thanks to God all the way to the town hall.

Charkey   Power to the people!

Lights.

Scene Three

Tuesday evening. Three weeks later. **Buster** *and* **Beatrice**'s *front room.* **Brendan, Elaine, Jane, Denzil, Charkey, Leonard** *sitting.* **John** *standing, thinking.*

John   Brendan.

Brendan   Yes, I agree with everyone else, you would make a good councillor.

John   As far as I am concerned I have failed to make the advice centre a success. Failure in the local election would be disastrous for me.

Elaine   Don't be silly, losing an election is not a failure.

Denzil   Who said he's going to lose? He was a very good disc jockey with his mouth before he opened the advice centre.

Charkey   But the man know everybody in the neighbourhood by their first and second name.

Jane   Yes, John, we need you to put some life into the community.

John   You know when Denzel, Len and Charkey first mentioned this political business to me, I thought it was a joke.

Brendan   The reason why you think it is a joke was because of the Rasta quotation.

Elaine   I don't mind which party he runs for so long as he don't join the Conservative Party and disgrace all of us.

Denzil   John is not a Conservative.

Leonard   How you know that? I see so many Black people change from one party to the next that I believe anything can happen.

Denzil   Just listen to yourself talking. This is supposed to be a political meeting where we are all supposed to be on the same side and follow the leader and John is the leader.

Charkey   I agree with Denzil.

Leonard   Brother John can speak for himself. Is him going to talk at the council meetings.

John   I am picking up some sense of sincerity and trust from all of you. So if I change my mind and consider myself running in the local elections I will have to reconstruct my life and it is a long time now since I was in a church.

Charkey   Then you must go, man. We don't want no heathen for our councillor.

Denzil   Brother John is going to church.

Leonard   Yes I think so too.

Jane   Probably this is the first time I am seeing the spiritual side of Black people.

John   Yes I'm going to go to church because it seems like you have to have God on your side before you can get any help for Black people.

Denzil   Yes the time has come to unify the community.

Elaine   John I really think you will make a good councillor.

John   Thanks.

Brendan   Does this mean you have decided?

John   Yes, I am going to go for it.

Jane   I am glad.

Uproar, laughter everybody shaking hands and clapping **John** *on the back. Enter* **Beatrice** *and* **Terrence**.

Beatrice   Hello, hello, hello. Good news I hope.

Jane   Yes, very good news.

Elaine   John is going to run in the local election.

Buster   Well, John, you feel good?

John   Yes, sir.

Buster   You have done a good thing to my heart now that you have decided to enter into real politics. Don't let them fool you, always wear a collar and tie. Let me shake your hand.

They shake hands, the lights dim and everybody goes into a trance, miming, discussing with each other, planning election campaign, **John** *miming political speech, others are writing in diaries and making appointments.* **Terrence** *is smiling at everyone – cannot follow discussion for two to four minutes.* **Beatrice** *claps her hands with rejoicement, everybody becomes normal.*

Beatrice   So, ladies and gentlemen, it just happen that over the last week I kept my ears to the ground and learn that this meeting might take place tonight so Terrence and myself have a little surprise for you. We're going to have a party. (*Party lights.*) Come with me, young Terrence. (*Exit* **Beatrice** *and* **Terrence**. *Spotlight on speaking character.*)

Buster   So how is the football team, Brendan?

Brendan   Oh, not bad. We won the last match.

Buster   The cup, man. I expect you'll win the cup.

Brendan   Yes, we probably could win if these three (*pointing at* **Denzil**, **Leonard** *and* **Charkey**) get stuck in.

Enter **Beatrice** *and* **Terrence** *with paper hats, one large rosette, bouquet of flowers, champagne glasses (flowers for* **Elaine**, *rosette for* **John** *and champagne for everyone) and paper hats. Exit* **Beatrice**. **Terrence** *opens champagne and serves to everyone.* **Beatrice** *re-enters with party food.*

Jane (*lights*)   To John.

Everybody   To John.

Buster   Well, I did not sit on my backside I did nothing while Beatrice was planning her party piece, I did my bit.

John   I know what that is and I'm sure everyone else knows as well.

Jane   Rum punch.

Buster   Yes, and I make the best rum punch in the world.

He exits quickly. Party lights. Spotlight on speaking character. **Terrence** *sips champagne, he doesn't like it. Everybody laughs.*

Beatrice   Elaine, how is everything at home?

Elaine   Oh much nicer since he realised he won't be able to carry on with the advice centre in the present situation.

Beatrice   Yes, I understand. So how do you feel about what he is doing now?

Elaine   Oh I support him all the way. We will be canvassing together.

Beatrice   Oh that's nice, I like that. He will make a good councillor. He was always tricky with his mouth.

Elaine   Oh, I know, no you don't have to tell me. (*They smile. Enter* **Buster** *with trays and glasses of rum punch for everyone, Coca-Cola for* **Terrence**.)

Brendan   And another toast to our future councillor.

Spotlight on **John**.

Everybody   To John. Cheers, cheers.

Spotlight on **Buster** *opening cabinet, showing lots more booze.*

Denzil   So how do you suggest we rally the brethrem them around brother John?

Charkey   Well, first we have to call a meeting and suggest the situation to the brethren them.

Leonard   Yes because the election is not that far away.

Denzil   That means that we have to start work as from tomorrow so therefore each one of us have to become the leader of a pack and rally the brethren them to go around in pairs knocking at people's doors asking them to vote for brother John.

Leonard   He will win the same way we are going to win the cup.

Denzil   One love.

Charkey   One love.

Leonard   Rasta for I.

John   Sorry I can't get through to your father, and not a word from your mother. Not much I can do, are you happy here?

Terrence   Yeh, I mean I don't want to go into council care, I am too old, I know the facts of life. Your mum and dad really nice. I would like to pay you back one day.

John   You already pay me back by being a good boy.

Terrence   I mean I know, nobody doesn't care anything about me, so I have to show my respect anywhere I find a little love. Your parents said I could stay as long as I want to.

John   Well, in the next month I will go and sort it out with the authority. If I don't get any sense out of your father Felix or find your mother. Is school holiday over yet?

Terrence   Next Monday we go back.

John   You must go back.

Terrence   I will.

John   That's right, keep going.

Jane   Nice food.

Beatrice   Thanks.

Jane   Buster rum punch is pretty potent.

Beatrice   Two spoonful of it always put me fast asleep.

Rama *at front door singing folk song, calypso style.*

> A lick him in him belly til him break him neck
> B lick him in him belly til him break him neck
> C lick him in him belly til him break him neck
> For the war a go start a Babylon yard
> For the war a go start a Babylon yard
> For the war a go start a Babylon yard
> For the Babylon yard is a rolling stone
> For the Babylon yard is a rolling stone
> For the Babylon yard is a rolling stone
> So D lick him in him belly til him break him neck
> So E lick him in him belly til him break him neck
> So F lick him in him belly til him break his neck
> For Babylon yard is a rolling stone

Lights – the party is over. **Rama** *continues singing in bass voice going through alphabet.* **Terrence** *exits quickly. Everybody waits for* **Rama** *to enter.* **Terrence** *and* **Rama** *enter,* **Rama** *carrying suitcase which he does not put down. He has been to* *barbers and had clean and shave retaining nice-shaped moustache. He is wearing suit and tie, with flowered shirt and flower in buttonhole.*

Rama   Scores of wild horses couldn't keep me away from here tonight. Oh yes, I remember this house, could be another headquarters. We will not just surprise the enemy this time, we shall teach them a very good lesson that never again the oppressors of South Africa and the men who collect the rates will ever reign again over our Black brothers in this small world which is my home. We are getting ready for the final assault. Road transport will be your job, John. You will not walk up the pearly gates of South Africa, you will be driven with columns of armoured vehicles and thousands or mire men deep abreast and behind.

Denzil   Rock of ages.

Charkey   Let me hide myself in thee.

Rama   So General Atlantic and his wonderful big oceans have finally cornered South Africa because the seas can never run dry.

Leonard   The right time is approaching the General's head.

Rama   So be it and let's move when the right time comes. Farewell until General Atlantic bombers are ready to fly and 'Dawn' will be the codename. See you at the pearly gates, John, with your band of soldiers and armoured transport.

John   Thank you, General.

Rama   Good luck.

He exits.

Buster   Tonight is got to be one of the most important night of my life. I'm very proud to know that this man John, my son will probably be in the position to speak up for some of us old poor Black folks.

John   First let me, let me assure everyone it is going to be sweet music for me from now on. What a glorious way to enter into politics. It is the first time all my immediate families and friends ever supported me at the same time in any of my adventures. Yes, we will win the election.

Brendan   Here, here.

Beatrice   You're saying it nicely, son.

Leonard   It feels good.

Buster   More rum punch for everybody?

Denzil   No, well, we're leaving now. Thank you just the same.

Charkey   Yes an early start to catch the brethren them in bed.

Denzil   So tomorrow's meeting is at the advice centre.

John   Yes.

Leonard   Night, everybody.

Exit **Charkey**, **Denzil** *and* **Leonard**.

Beatrice   Right, Terrence, it's bed for you as well.

She exits, **Terrence** *follows.*

Brendan   Yes I'm leaving as well. Nice party. Nice evening. We are sure to win.

John   Thank you for your support.

Brendan   You're doing a good job.

Elaine   See you tomorrow.

Brendan   Yes.

He exit.

Buster   So tell me, John, have you ever voted? You know I always voted for the Iron Lady party.

John   I never take any notice of your political ideas.

Elaine   Yes, we voted, always for the Labour candidate.

Buster   So you're Labour candidate?

John   No, independent. It is too late to get on the Labour bandwagon, perhaps later I will join the Labour Party. Let's see what they have to offer.

Jane   Buster, I'm surprised you're not a socialist.

Buster   Well, in the war Mr Churchill was my man, I haven't changed. That's why I follow the Iron Lady. Is one advice I have to offer you, John. Don't get left in the cold, get in the middle and fight like hell to get on top.

Jane   He will.

Elaine   He's on the right track this time.

Buster   Well, if I'm going to vote for him he's got to be on the right track.

Beatrice *enters.*

Beatrice   Come on, Buster, let's go to bed. John you have made the right decision. Elaine, are you staying here tonight?

Elaine   Yes.

Jane   Right, see you two bright and early in the morning. Beatrice, Buster, thank you very much for a nice evening. Your rum punch is something else. I will see myself out. Night.

Buster   Thanks. Have you find out who take the money from the safe?

Elaine   He left it in the kitchen at home. I nearly threw it away in the dustbin by mistake.

Buster   That's good.

Beatrice   I am glad. Come let me kiss you, son. (*She kisses* **John**.) Goodnight.

Elaine   Goodnight.

Exit **Buster** *and* **Beatrice**.

John   I am glad I got your support.

Elaine   That's the least I could do after all those lean years.

John   I am putting on a brave face but I'm really very nervous.

Elaine   Well, it all happened so quickly. I can feel a wind of change is blowing over Kilburn.

John   You think so?

Elaine   Yes. You're an important man in the community and deep down you're a good person, a bit stupid sometimes, but nevertheless a likeable person.

John   I hope all my stupidity is behind me now that I'm climbing the ladder.

Elaine   You show great strength since you start thinking about running in this election.

John   You still love me?

Elaine   Of course I do.

John   Let's go to bed.

Elaine   And win the election.

John   Praise the Lord!

End.

Weekend Lovers

Characters

Jim, *born in England of Caribbean and European parents, middle twenties, office clerk*
Kathleen, *born in England of Caribbean and European parents, middle twenties, office clerk*
Frank, *Black-English, late twenties, office clerk*
Angela, *White-English, late twenties, office clerk*
Sherry, *White-English, middle thirties, housewife*
Dennis, *White-English, late thirties, pub landlord*

Scene One

*In **Jim** and **Kathleen**'s flat. **Jim** is up and dressed, **Kathleen** is still in bed. They are in the middle of a discussion.*

Jim   We have got our own flat.

Kathleen   What do you mean? Please turn off the music.

Music is turned off.

Jim   What is wrong with you this weekend?

Kathleen   The same thing for the last six months, or perhaps you haven't noticed.

Jim   Six months ago we were living in a damp, cold room.

Kathleen   I feel trapped in this cul-de-sac of a place.

Jim   What do you propose we do, have a party?

Kathleen   It wouldn't help the situation, it only depresses me.

Jim   I was only joking.

Kathleen   We're only young once, let's get out of this ghetto type of life.

Jim   Majority of young people are worse off than us. We both have a job in the same department.

Kathleen   Don't try to pull wool over my eyes. I don't care about the bloody job. I want a better life than this drawn-out drama every weekend.

Jim   Should I go and score some dope?

Kathleen   No.

Jim   Do you want to come for a drink?

Kathleen   No.

Jim   What do you want?

Kathleen   Nothing, nothing and everything. What are we going to do this weekend?

Jim   Well, for a start I'm going to have a good drink and go back to work on Monday morning.

Kathleen   I am not going back to any work until my head gets into a higher plane.

Jim   I just don't like negative energy. I like to think positive. Why are you making yourself so sad when there's nothing to be sad about.

Kathleen   For God sake stop sitting on a cloud of dope with your face buried in the ground.

Jim   I am going for a drink.

Kathleen   No, listen something is wrong.

Jim   I love you, that is all that matters.

Kathleen   Why because we are both half-castes?

Jim   No, what's wrong with you this morning, Kathleen?

Kathleen   It's not morning. It is one o'clock in the afternoon. We were bloody drunk again last night. Jesus Christ, nearly all the money we only spent buying dope and booze.

Jim   Those two commodities have helped us out of some tight spots in the past.

Kathleen   Well, the past has nothing to do with this weekend's lonely feelings. You go off and do the same rubbish every weekend.

Jim   You can't have a future without the help of the past.

Kathleen   Don't lecture me, talk to me properly. You are not my psychiatrist.

Jim   I didn't know you had one.

Kathleen   I'll be seeing one if this continues much longer.

Jim   Are you mad?

Kathleen   No.

Jim   So why do you need a psychiatrist?

Kathleen   So he or she can stop me from going mad.

Jim   Are you serious?

Kathleen   Yes.

Jim   But you smoke twice as much dope as myself, so you don't need no psychiatrist.

Kathleen   Haven't you noticed, I stopped smoking. I only used to smoke because you live in the pub when you're not working.

Jim   I don't follow your point.

Kathleen   Why can't you follow what I'm saying?

Jim   Just calm down.

Kathleen   You're the one who needs calming down.

Jim   I am going for a drink.

Kathleen   Yes, keep on running away as soon as we were talking about anything that concerns facts. I don't know why you don't put on a pair of shorts and go for a run.

Jim   Good idea, but first I must have a drink.

Kathleen   Oh please yourself, don't be surprised about my future conduct.

Jim   Are you threatening me?

Kathleen   How could I possibly do that?

Jim   Lots of different ways.

Kathleen   Name me one.

Jim   If you don't know, I'm not going to tell you.

Kathleen   Let's go to the sports shop and buy a couple of pairs of tracksuits, and then think about going for a run in the park.

Jim   When are you going to have the time and energy to go running in the park?

Kathleen   We could do it right now if you weren't going to the pub.

Jim   Don't be daft, let's talk about this in bed tomorrow.

Kathleen   Suppose I'm not here tomorrow?

Jim   No psychiatrist is going to send you away before Monday.

Kathleen   We could never talk properly in bed since we moved here because your head is always full of booze or dope.

Jim   Do me a favour, cut the crap.

Kathleen   Oh go to hell and leave me alone.

Jim   Right, I'll see you later. Are you sure you don't want any dope for the weekend?

Kathleen   Bollocks.

Jim   Naughty, naughty.

Kathleen   Get out of here, you bloody drunkard.

Jim   As you wish, my lady.

Kathleen   Piss off I tell you before I kill you.

Scene Two

A public house.

Dennis   Hey, what's happening Jim, you're a bit late. Is the missus putting her foot down? Or did you have one too many last night?

Jim   Both.

Dennis   Right, what's your pleasure? Pint of lager?

Jim   And a large scotch. What's happening this weekend?

Dennis   Nothing special, disco and go-go dancing.

Jim   Kathleen is driving me mad.

Dennis   Yeh, how comes?

Jim   She wants us to get out of the ghetto.

Dennis   What ghetto? You don't live in a ghetto do you?

Jim   Kathleen thinks differently.

Dennis   Has she gone queer or something?

Jim   She wants us to turn our backs on the place we were born and go and live with plastic people somewhere else in London.

Dennis   Is she pregnant?

Jim   No I don't think so.

Dennis   So, she's getting posh is she?

Jim   Worse than that, she wants us to give up smoking and go running.

Dennis   Be careful, don't allow her to wear the trousers.

Jim   I don't care what she wears, but why start calling our nice friendly neighbourhood a ghetto. I certainly don't have the attitude of a ghetto person.

Sherry *enters.*

Sherry   Hello, Dennis, Jim.

Jim   Hi, Sherry.

Dennis   Gin and tonic?

Sherry   Yes, please. Where is everybody?

Dennis   At home watching the game.

Sherry   Oh yes, another day of television sport.

Dennis   I wasn't going to open the pub until late afternoon.

Sherry   That would be against the law, isn't it.

Dennis   I don't know.

Sherry   You should find out the next time you apply for a licence. Cheer up, Jim, what is the matter, such a long face.

Jim   Kathleen is having a go at me and I don't know if I should take her seriously or not.

Sherry   Why can't you take her seriously?

Dennis   Yes, sir, pint of Guinness and half a bitter shandy.

Jim   Dennis, can you speak deaf and dumb language?

Dennis   No. No one can speak it.

Jim   Clever. I mean do you understand it?

Sherry   No, he doesn't understand deaf and dumb language. That's what they always have.

Jim   Oh yes, that's right.

Sherry   Any requests? I'm going to put on some music.

Jim   No, just play something nice of your own choice.

Music comes on. Shirley Bassey singing 'something'.

Scene Three

Kathleen *and* **Jim** *'s flat.* **Kathleen** *dialling on the telephone.*

Angela   Hello.

Kathleen   Hello, Angie.

Angela   Hello, Kathleen what's up?

Kathleen   He has gone to the pub.

Angela   Doesn't he understand or care about his health?

Kathleen   I am worried for me.

Angela   Does he?

Kathleen   I don't know. Have you seen Frank?

Angela   Yes, but why?

Kathleen   No buts, where is he?

Angela   Are you sure about this?

Kathleen   Yes I am sure. What's his number? Jim's got it somewhere here but I can't find it.

Angela   You know he's got a girlfriend.

Kathleen   I don't care.

Angela   Come on, give Jim a chance. Don't start making snap decisions.

Kathleen   It is not a snap decision. I am definitely getting out of this hell hole.

Angela   Come on, what's happened this morning between you two?

Kathleen   Nothing, just the same old story.

Angela   Okay. Let's meet in town this afternoon.

Kathleen   Well. Yes. Sure. Let's talk some more before we decide where to meet.

Angela   Why are you crying?

Kathleen   I don't think I love Jim anymore. I already started packing.

Angela   What! Shall I come over?

Kathleen   Yes please, I could do with an extra hand.

Angela   Look, I like Jim. I'm not going to help you to leave him.

Kathleen   Please, I need time to sort out my head.

Angela   I will come over in ten minutes.

Kathleen   Yes. Thanks. News time. (*Turns wireless on.*)

Wireless: Good afternoon, this is the two o'clock news. MPs are sitting again all night in the House debating the long bill. The prime minister is extremely concerned about the problem of glue sniffing amongst the young.

Kathleen   No. God have mercy. (*She switches off wireless.*)

Scene Four

Back at the pub.

Sherry   What makes you think women are as strong as men?

Jim   I know Kathleen. She's a tough cookie. Another large scotch, Dennis, please.

Dennis   Take it's easy, it's only 2 o'clock.

Jim   I am taking it easy. She should be here by now. She always follows me anywhere I go.

Sherry   Come on, sweetie, give her a call and tell her you love her.

Jim   Why should I have to tell her that I love her?

Dennis   Because you do.

Jim   Where is my scotch? What are you having, Sherry?

Sherry   I am not feeling very well. Orange juice please.

Jim   You sure?

Sherry   Yes.

Jim   Dennis?

Dennis   Nothing for me, thank you.

Money goes into the jukebox. Bob Marley singing 'One Love' in the background.

Jim   Thanks, Dennis, how much is that?

Dennis   One ninety.

Jim   Sherry, do you think I've got a ghetto mentality?

Sherry   No, I think you are more of the middle-class type. Well, you're different from your father aren't you?

Jim   What do you mean?

Sherry   Well, he's an Oriental gentleman isn't he?

Jim   But my mother is white.

Sherry   So?

Jim   Kathleen thinks I should give up smoking dope.

Sherry   Well, for goodness sake what's wrong with that?

Jim   Nothing, except she smokes as well. Well she used to.

Sherry   It is time for a change. The police are cracking down on all the drug dens.

Jim   What's wrong with smoking a bit of dope?

Sherry   Makes you lazy.

Jim   I go to work every day except Saturday and Sunday.

Sherry   I mean in your head.

Jim   This is getting too much for me. Perhaps you are right as well.

Sherry   Sorry?

Jim   It's not your fault.

Sherry   Come on, have a heart. Why did you leave her on her own at home?

Jim   Bad habit I suppose. Dennis, another large scotch please.

Dennis   No, Jim. Go and look for Kathleen, you know you're not happy unless you are with her.

Sherry   Yes, that's a good idea.

Jim   No fear, I am staying put.

Sherry   Darling, you're old enough.

Jim   I am willing to give up smoking dope if it will help the situation.

Sherry   You have made a good decision. Don't let don't ruin your marriage.

Jim   Dennis, did Frank come in this morning?

Dennis   No.

Jim   Can I use your phone?

Dennis   Sure.

He dials.

Jim   Hi, Frank.

Frank   Hello, Jim.

Jim   Are you coming out for a drink?

Frank   No, probably tonight. I'm going running this afternoon.

Jim   When did you take up running?

Frank   Six weeks ago.

Jim   What's wrong with everybody?

Frank   What do you mean?

Jim   Where are you going for a run?

Frank   In the park. Would you like to come?

Jim   I will come and watch while I'm drinking my scotch.

Frank   Angie tells me that you and Kathleen were going to take up running.

Jim   Kathleen mentioned something like that this morning.

Frank   She given up smoking?

Jim   Well, she hasn't smoked for a few days.

Frank   Bravo. I haven't touched a cigarette or dope for sixteen days. What about yourself, have you given up?

Jim   Are you serious?

Frank   Well, it's up to you.

Jim   Listen, man, would you and Angie like to come over for a meal this evening?

Frank   Sure, I will give her a bell.

Scene Five

Kathleen *and* **Jim** *'s flat.*

Angela   Now tell me all about it.

Kathleen   I am ready to leave him.

Angela   No you are not. I am going to help you unpack this silly little weekend bag. Come on, stop crying.

Kathleen   I can't.

Angela   Frank and Jim are friends.

Kathleen   No they are not. Frank is different.

Angela   Darling, they are both men.

Kathleen   What kind of advice is that?

Angela   You can't just pack up and leave like this.

Kathleen   That is the only way he's going to know how serious I am about smoking and drinking and this bloody ghetto life. These six streets around here are the bloodiest front line of the world. One minute you're happy and the next minute you're down in the dumps. He can't see what this place is doing to our marriage. Frank didn't buy a flat here, he went off somewhere else. He's twice as sensible as Jim.

Angela   No he's not. Jim is just a happy-go-lucky guy. There, all neatly packed away in your wardrobe. You weren't taking a lot with you were you.

Kathleen   No, thanks, Angie. You know I said to him, 'Let's buy a couple of tracksuits and go running'. He thinks I was mad and he left instantly for the pub.

Angela   You shouldn't tell him anything. Just go out and buy two pair of tracksuits. Come on, pull yourself together and think straight. Let's go for a walk later this afternoon and look at a few sports shops.

Kathleen   You think it's going to work out between Jim and myself?

Angela   Of course it will.

Kathleen   But he will have to change.

Angela   Come on, let's get into a better mood. Don't forget you love him, that's why you're so worried.

Kathleen   You know that Frank's girlfriend that you were telling me about, is that girlfriend you, Angie?

Angela   Yes.

Kathleen   When did it happen?

Angela   Since we started running together. And it is a full two weeks now since we started sleeping together.

Kathleen   I am always the last person to know anything.

Angela   It is no secret.

Key turns in the door.

Here he comes, pull yourself together.

Kathleen   All right, I'll try.

Jim   Hello, Angie.

Angela   Hi, Jim.

Jim   Surprise, surprise.

Angela   Why?

Jim   No reason, I can smell something is wrong.

Angela   Don't be so pessimistic.

Kathleen   Drunk again.

Jim   No I am not

Kathleen   Are you thinking seriously about what I was telling you this morning?

Jim   I have no other choice.

Kathleen   Good. Angie and myself are going shopping.

Jim   Yeh, all right.

Kathleen   Come on Angie, let's go.

Angela   See you later, Jim.

Jim   No, wait a minute. I'm going to get a meal together. I asked Frank to come over. He was going to phone you, Angie.

Angela   Oh, was he?

Jim   I might as well ask you for him.

Angela   Yes, I see. Yes all right.

Jim   Do you still eat meat?

Angela   Not very much.

Jim   What about roast chicken?

Angela   Yes, all right.

Scene Six

*In **Kathleen** and **Jim**'s flat. **Jim** is in bed. **Kathleen** is fully dressed in a tracksuit.*

Kathleen   Come on, Jim, wake up.

Jim   What?

Kathleen   Wake up.

Jim   All right, all right, I'm awake.

Kathleen   Try these on.

Jim   What is it?

Kathleen   Tracksuit and jogging shoes, come on put them on.

Jim   Yes, all right. Give me a chance to open my eyes. What time is it?

Kathleen   Dawn, the best time for a run.

Jim   What about a cup of coffee before we go?

Kathleen   No, come on before the sun comes up.

Jim   I can't function on a Sunday morning without a joint.

Kathleen   Yes you can. Come on, we're going to meet up with Frank and Angie in the park.

Jim   Do they have anything to do with this punishment?

Kathleen   Yes. Are you going to put on the tracksuit?

Jim   Yes, all right.

He puts on tracksuit.

Kathleen   You like them?

Jim   Yeh, a bit jazzy.

Kathleen   Good, and we're going to sell this flat and move somewhere else.

Jim   Why?

Kathleen   Because I'm tired of hiding from police when we're going into basement hole to buy dope. Why should we have to go to prison for spending our own money?

Jim   It is not bad as that.

Kathleen   Yes it is and worse.

Jim   But everybody is so friendly around here.

Kathleen   Yes, until something goes wrong. Then it becomes a death trap.

Jim   Are you sure about this running lark?

Kathleen   Yes, you never know until you try.

Doorbell.

Jim   I will get it.

Frank   Wow, you look great in them tracksuit, man.

Jim   You think so?

Angela   Yes, very nice.

Kathleen   I thought we were going to meet you in the park.

Frank   Well, we decided to come over and get him out of bed just in case he wasn't strong enough to persuade him.

Kathleen   Judge for yourself.

Angela   He looks willing and ready to me.

Jim   What is this?

Frank   Nothing, man, just our good intentions.

Kathleen   Thanks, Frank.

Angela   Are we ready?

Kathleen   I am.

Frank   So, Jim, how far do you think you'll be able to run this morning?

Jim   I don't know. I'm just a pawn in your plan.

Front door closes. All four walking along corridor.

Kathleen   I can do a mile, but I'm sure Jim could do two or three miles. Here goes the champion of champions.

Jim   Life is really amazing.

Frank   Sure thing, brother.

Jim   This is a brand new leaf. Let's shake ourselves up before we get into the park.

They all start running along and laughing.

End.

Alfred Fagon

Juliet Gilkes Romero

Of art, Nina Simone, the singer and civil rights icon, said: 'You can't help it. An artist's duty is to reflect the times.'

I think of this quote when I think of Jamaican Alfred Fagon. Like Simone, Fagon's work is defiant, unflinching. He authored seven plays. All are politically fearless. This is not a man who worried about the good opinion of others. I admire his confidence, fire and perseverance. Theatre can be an unforgiving industry where Black writers are often not given the room to evolve and take risks and grow from creative challenge. This is how careers are often extinguished. In the seventies, Fagon's work was being performed at Hampstead Theatre and the Royal Court. He was writing for BBC Drama. *Shakespeare's Country* was filmed for BBC 2. He was creatively on fire. Writers today would benefit enormously from his experience, perspective and advice. I know I would.

Not only was Fagon a stage-screenwriter. He was a poet and an actor. His black and white photos show a fit, radiant man with the hint of a wry humorous smile. His military service was with the Royal Signals, the same regiment as my father. They were about the same age. Both had plenty to say about the world they lived in, racial justice and civil rights. Both loved cricket and understood the profound cultural significance of West Indian cricket glory for the Windrush generation. This is evident in *The Death of a Black Man.* The confidence of the main protagonist, Shakie, is driven by his love of the West Indies cricket team and their legendary captain Garfield Sobers. 'Black people jumping for joy all over England. Black people is the best cricketers in the world and Sobers is their captain,' he declares.

It's hard to comprehend how Fagon, whose star was burning so bright, collapsed and died alone in a residential street and was then shamefully given a hurried and anonymous pauper's burial despite the police searching his flat and failing to notice his passport, letters and BBC script next to his bed. The details are disturbing and well known now but the flagrant disregard for his dignity, the dignity he championed in his writing for all in the West Indian diaspora, should never be forgotten.

And like the Dutch painter Vincent van Gogh, the African American writer Zora Neale Hurston and singer Otis Redding, Fagon was ultimately destined to find renown posthumously and certainly with the launch of the Alfred Fagon Award. The prize has been won by trailblazing Black British writers, including Michaela Coel. I wonder what Fagon would make of *I May Destroy You,* Coel's breath taking exploration of consent, race and millennial life.

I wonder what Fagon would have made of the global Black Lives Matter movement and the racist murder of George Floyd.

Fagon's artistic provocations carved their own unblinking signature on British theatre by capturing the texture and political reality of the Windrush generation, long before the term erupted into public consciousness and TV news bulletins following the contemptible mistreatment of so many of its descendants who had lawfully made their lives in Britain.

It's high time that Fagon is better known not just for the prize in his name but for his prolific body of work achieved before his untimely death at the age of forty-nine. Fagon deserves to be remembered as one of the most important and influential Black writers in this country, and as someone who pursued the artistic freedom to reflect the times in which he lived. Thankfully, all seven of his plays have now been published. I wish I had known Fagon and was honoured to win the Alfred Fagon Award. I hope to help keep his legacy burning bright.